Simple Suppers

Jean Paré

www.companyscoming.com
visit our website

Front Cover

1. Walnut Green Salad, page 12
2. Pork Marsala, page 134

Props courtesy of: Pfaltzgraff Canada

Back Cover

1. Pecan Potato Salad, page 23
2. Seafood Spinach Salad, page 37
3. Sun-Dried Tomato Crostini, page 59

Props courtesy of: Totally Bamboo

Eleventh Printing March 2011

Library and Archives Canada Cataloguing in Publication
Paré, Jean, date
Simple suppers / Jean Paré.
(Original series)
Includes index.
ISBN 978-1-897069-14-1
1. Suppers. 2. Quick and easy cookery. I. Title.
II. Series: Paré, Jean, date- Original series.
TX738.P37 2007   641.5'38   C2006-905121-6

We gratefully acknowledge the following suppliers for their generous support of our Test and Photography Kitchens:

Broil King Barbecues
Hamilton Beach® Canada
Proctor Silex® Canada
Corelle®
Lagostina®
Tupperware®

Published by
Company's Coming Publishing Limited
2311 – 96 Street
Edmonton, Alberta, Canada T6N 1G3
Tel: 780-450-6223   Fax: 780-450-1857
www.companyscoming.com

Company's Coming is a registered trademark owned by Company's Coming Publishing Limited

We acknowledge the financial support of the Government of Canada through the Canada Book Fund for our publishing activities.

Printed in China

Get more great recipes...FREE!

click

search

print

cook

From apple pie to zucchini bread, we've got you covered. Browse our free online recipes for Guaranteed Great!™ results.

You can also sign up to receive our **FREE online newsletter**. You'll receive exclusive offers, FREE recipes & cooking tips, new title previews, and much more...all delivered to your in-box.

So don't delay, visit our website today!

www.companyscoming.com
visit our ↖ website

Company's Coming Cookbooks

Quick & easy recipes; everyday ingredients!

Original Series

- Softcover, 160 pages
- Lay-flat plastic comb binding
- Full-colour photos
- Nutrition information

Original Series

- Softcover, 160 pages
- Lay-flat plastic comb binding
- Full-colour photos
- Nutrition information

2-in-1 Cookbook Collection

- Softcover, 256 pages
- Lay-flat plastic coil binding
- Full-colour photos
- Nutrition information

Original Series

- Softcover, 160 pages
- Lay-flat plastic comb binding
- Full-colour photos
- Updated format

For a complete listing of our cookbooks, visit our website:
www.companyscoming.com

Table of Contents

Side Salads

Meal Salads

Side Dishes

Beef

Chicken

Fish & Seafood

Lamb

Meatless

Pork

The Company's Coming Story

Jean Paré (pronounced "jeen PAIR-ee") grew up understanding that the combination of family, friends and home cooking is the best recipe for a good life. From her mother, she learned to appreciate good cooking, while her father praised even her earliest attempts in the kitchen. When Jean left home, she took with her a love of cooking, many family recipes and an intriguing desire to read cookbooks as if they were novels!

"Never share a recipe you wouldn't use yourself." When her four children had all reached school age, Jean volunteered to cater the 50th anniversary celebration of the Vermilion School of Agriculture, now Lakeland College, in Alberta, Canada. Working out of her home, Jean prepared a dinner for more than 1,000 people, launching a flourishing catering operation that continued for over 18 years. During that time, she had countless opportunities to test new ideas with immediate feedback—resulting in empty plates and contented customers! Whether preparing cocktail sandwiches for a house party or serving a hot meal for 1,500 people, Jean Paré earned a reputation for great food, courteous service and reasonable prices.

As requests for her recipes increased, Jean was often asked the question, "Why don't you write a cookbook?" Jean responded by teaming up with her son, Grant Lovig, in the fall of 1980 to form Company's Coming Publishing Limited. The publication of *150 Delicious Squares* on April 14, 1981 marked the debut of what would soon become one of the world's most popular cookbook series.

The company has grown since those early days when Jean worked from a spare bedroom in her home. Today, she continues to write recipes while working closely with the staff of the Recipe Factory, as the Company's Coming test kitchen is affectionately known.

There she fills the role of mentor, assisting with the development of recipes people most want to use for everyday cooking and easy entertaining. Every Company's Coming recipe is *kitchen-tested* before it is approved for publication.

Jean's daughter, Gail Lovig, is responsible for marketing and distribution, leading a team that includes sales personnel located in major cities across Canada. Company's Coming cookbooks are distributed in Canada, the United States, Australia and other world markets. Bestsellers many times over in English, Company's Coming cookbooks have also been published in French and Spanish.

Familiar and trusted in home kitchens around the world, Company's Coming cookbooks are offered in a variety of formats. Highly regarded as kitchen workbooks, the softcover Original Series, with its lay-flat plastic comb binding, is still a favourite among readers.

Jean Paré's approach to cooking has always called for *quick and easy recipes* using *everyday ingredients.* That view has served her well. The recipient of many awards, including the Queen Elizabeth Golden Jubilee Medal, Jean was appointed Member of the Order of Canada, her country's highest lifetime achievement honour.

Jean continues to gain new supporters by adhering to what she calls The Golden Rule of Cooking: *Never share a recipe you wouldn't use yourself.* It's an approach that has worked—*millions of times over!*

Foreword

Good things, they say, come in threes—cheers, wishes and wise men, to name, well, three—so it stands to reason that an easy way to organize a delicious dinner is to think in terms of that magical number.

Simple Suppers does just that. It breaks meal-planning down to a trio of necessary elements: vegetables, starches and proteins. Put all three on a plate and you have a full-meal deal that will make a nutritionist smile. What makes this Company's Coming cookbook special, however, is that we've told you how to combine those three elements so you can serve a great-tasting, well-balanced supper every time.

We've divided our table of contents into—you guessed it—three categories: salads, sides and entrees. Some of our meal salads are easy, one-dish meals that are completely balanced on their own. You'll find similarly balanced options in our entree section.

Of course, we also offer a number of tasty one and two-component recipes—all with helpful suggestions on how to incorporate them into a balanced meal. You can follow our suggested combinations or add your own family favourites to create a more personalized dinner medley of vegetables, starch and protein. Our Salmon With

Avocado Salsa, for instance, pairs perfectly with our Chipotle Cheese Potatoes from the sides section. And our heavenly Pork Marsala, for example, goes well with your own buttered egg noodles and our Walnut Green Salad for an elegant, guest-friendly dinner.

Each section features all-new recipes prepared in a number of different ways, whether baked, grilled, tossed or cooked on top of the stove. And to keep things really simple, we've made sure that every dish is quick to prepare, so you can get on with your evening.

Now that deserves three cheers!

Jean Paré

Nutrition Information Guidelines

Each recipe is analyzed using the most current version of the Canadian Nutrient File from Health Canada, which is based on the United States Department of Agriculture (USDA) Nutrient Database.

- If more than one ingredient is listed (such as "butter or hard margarine"), or if a range is given (1 – 2 tsp., 5 – 10 mL), only the first ingredient or first amount is analyzed.
- For meat, poultry and fish, the serving size per person is based on the recommended 4 oz. (113 g) uncooked weight (without bone), which is 2 – 3 oz. (57 – 85 g) cooked weight (without bone)—approximately the size of a deck of playing cards.
- Milk used is 1% M.F. (milk fat), unless otherwise stated.

- Cooking oil used is canola oil, unless otherwise stated.
- Ingredients indicating "sprinkle," "optional," or "for garnish" are not included in the nutrition information.
- The fat in recipes and combination foods can vary greatly depending on the sources and types of fats used in each specific ingredient. For these reasons, the amount of saturated, monounsaturated and polyunsaturated fats may not add up to the total fat content.

Vera C. Mazurak, Ph.D.
Nutritionist

Marinated Mushroom Salad

Not "mushroom" on your dinner table? You'll want to make some once you get a glimpse of this eye-catching, Asian-style salad. Marinate the mushrooms while preparing Italian Steak Dinner, page 77. Serve with foccacia bread on the side.

Rice vinegar	3 tbsp.	50 mL
Olive (or cooking) oil	1 tbsp.	15 mL
Soy sauce	1 tbsp.	15 mL
Sesame oil	2 tsp.	10 mL
Olive (or cooking) oil	1 tsp.	5 mL
Halved fresh white mushrooms	8 cups	2 L
Thinly sliced English cucumber (with peel)	1 1/2 cups	375 mL
Finely chopped green onion	2 tbsp.	30 mL
Olive (or cooking) oil	1 1/2 tbsp.	25 mL
Dijon mustard	1 tsp.	5 mL
Mixed salad greens, lightly packed	6 cups	1.5 L
Sesame seeds, toasted (see Tip, page 20)	2 tbsp.	30 mL

Combine first 4 ingredients in small cup. Set aside.

Heat second amount of olive oil in large frying pan on medium. Add mushrooms. Cook for about 10 minutes, stirring occasionally, until softened. Transfer to medium bowl.

Add 2 tbsp. (30 mL) rice vinegar mixture, cucumber and green onion. Toss. Chill for 1 hour.

Add third amount of olive oil and mustard to remaining rice vinegar mixture. Stir.

Put salad greens into large bowl. Drizzle with mustard mixture. Toss. Arrange on 4 large plates. Top with mushroom mixture.

Sprinkle with sesame seeds. Makes 4 salads. Serves 4.

1 serving: 185 Calories; 14.8 g Total Fat (8.8 g Mono, 3.1 g Poly, 2.0 g Sat); 0 mg Cholesterol; 10 g Carbohydrate; 4 g Fibre; 7 g Protein; 376 mg Sodium

Asparagus Cucumber Salad

Smoky grilled asparagus and crisp cucumber make a winning combination in this refreshing sweet and sour salad. Makes a great complement for Satay Chicken Noodles, page 80, or Asian Salmon Burgers, page 104.

Brown sugar, packed	2 tbsp.	30 mL
Mayonnaise	1 tbsp.	15 mL
Soy sauce	1 tbsp.	15 mL
Sesame (or cooking) oil	1 tbsp.	15 mL
Rice vinegar	1 tbsp.	15 mL
Finely grated gingerroot (or 1/4 tsp., 1 mL, ground ginger)	1 tsp.	5 mL
Pepper	1/4 tsp.	1 mL
Fresh asparagus, trimmed of tough ends, cut into 2 inch (5 cm) pieces	1 lb.	454 g
Thinly sliced English cucumber (with peel)	2 cups	500 mL
Sesame seeds, toasted (see Tip, page 20)	1 tsp.	5 mL

Whisk first 7 ingredients in small cup. Set aside.

Cook asparagus in boiling water in covered medium saucepan for 2 to 3 minutes until tender-crisp. Cool under cold running water. Put into medium bowl.

Add cucumber. Toss. Drizzle mayonnaise mixture over salad. Toss.

Sprinkle with sesame seeds. Makes about 3 1/2 cups (875 mL). Serves 4.

1 serving: 122 Calories; 6.8 g Total Fat (3.0 g Mono, 2.6 g Poly, 0.9 g Sat); 2 mg Cholesterol; 15 g Carbohydrate; 2 g Fibre; 3 g Protein; 353 mg Sodium

SMOKY ASPARAGUS SALAD: Preheat gas barbecue to medium. Cook uncut asparagus spears on greased grill for about 5 minutes, turning several times until tender-crisp. Cut into 2 inch (5 cm) pieces.

Pictured on page 107.

Dijon Apple Coleslaw

Apples add a fresh, summery appeal to this crisp, di-jaunty coleslaw. A good match for grilled chicken, beef or pork patties. Add grilled polenta slices for a complete meal.

Mayonnaise	1/4 cup	60 mL
Plain yogurt	1/4 cup	60 mL
Dijon mustard	1 tbsp.	15 mL
Apple cider vinegar	2 tsp.	10 mL
Granulated sugar	2 tsp.	10 mL
Salt	1/4 tsp.	1 mL
Pepper	1/8 tsp.	0.5 mL
Coleslaw mix (about 1 lb., 454 g)	8 cups	2 L
Grated peeled apple	1 cup	250 mL

Combine first 7 ingredients in large bowl.

Add coleslaw and apple. Toss. Makes about 6 cups (1.5 L). Serves 6.

1 serving: 113 Calories; 7.8 g Total Fat (4.2 g Mono, 2.5 g Poly, 0.9 g Sat); 7 mg Cholesterol; 9 g Carbohydrate; 2 g Fibre; 1.5 g Protein; 207 mg Sodium

Grated Carrot Salad

Don't pine away for want of a good side salad! This sweet and tangy carrot slaw is made intriguingly unique with the crunch of toasted pine nuts. A lovely side for Ground Pork Patties, page 145, and mashed potatoes.

Grated carrot	1 1/2 cups	375 mL
Chopped celery	1/4 cup	60 mL
Golden raisins	1/4 cup	60 mL
Pine nuts, toasted (see Tip, page 20)	2 tbsp.	30 mL
Chopped green onion	2 tbsp.	30 mL
HONEY MUSTARD VINAIGRETTE		
Cooking oil	1 tbsp.	15 mL
White vinegar	2 tsp.	10 mL
Liquid honey	2 tsp.	10 mL
Prepared mustard	1 tsp.	5 mL
Salt	1/4 tsp.	1 mL

(continued on next page)

Put first 5 ingredients into medium bowl. Toss.

Honey Mustard Vinaigrette: Combine all 5 ingredients in jar with tight-fitting lid. Shake well. Makes about 2 tbsp. (30 mL) vinaigrette. Drizzle over salad. Toss. Makes about 2 cups (500 mL) salad. Serves 4.

1 serving: 121 Calories; 6.1 g Total Fat (3.0 g Mono, 2.2 g Poly, 0.7 g Sat); 0 mg Cholesterol; 16 g Carbohydrate; 3 g Fibre; 2 g Protein; 197 mg Sodium

---

Sweet Potato Salad

Spicy, sweet and succulent, this curried potato salad will be an all-star at the family picnic. Makes a marvelous match for Pineapple Pork Kabobs, page 135.

Unpeeled sweet potatoes (or yams), halved crosswise	1 1/2 lbs.	680 g
Chopped green pepper	1/2 cup	125 mL
DRESSING		
Plain yogurt	2 tbsp.	30 mL
Mayonnaise	1 tbsp.	15 mL
Mango chutney, finely chopped	1 tbsp.	15 mL
Frozen concentrated orange juice, thawed	1 1/2 tsp.	7 mL
Curry powder	1/4 tsp.	1 mL
Ground cumin	1/4 tsp.	1 mL
Salt	1/8 tsp.	0.5 mL
Pepper	1/8 tsp.	0.5 mL

Cook sweet potato in boiling salted water in large saucepan until just tender. Drain. Rinse with cold water. Drain well. Remove peel. Cut sweet potato into 1/2 inch (12 mm) pieces. Put into medium bowl.

Add green pepper. Toss.

Dressing: Combine all 8 ingredients in small cup. Add to salad. Toss. Makes about 4 cups (1 L). Serves 4.

1 serving: 223 Calories; 3.6 g Total Fat (1.6 g Mono, 1.2 g Poly, 0.6 g Sat); 3 mg Cholesterol; 45 g Carbohydrate; 6 g Fibre; 3 g Protein; 105 mg Sodium

Walnut Green Salad

Your guests will go nuts for this tangy, crisp and crunchy salad. The citrus vinaigrette makes it a natural fit with Pork Marsala, page 134, and mashed potatoes or rice.

CITRUS BALSAMIC VINAIGRETTE

Balsamic vinaigrette	1/3 cup	75 mL
Orange juice	2 tbsp.	30 mL
Finely chopped green onion	2 tbsp.	30 mL
Grated orange zest	1/4 tsp.	1 mL

SALAD

Mixed salad greens, lightly packed	4 cups	1 L
Fresh spinach leaves, stems removed, lightly packed	4 cups	1 L
Can of mandarin orange segments, drained	10 oz.	284 mL
Thinly sliced radish	1 cup	250 mL
Coarsely chopped walnuts, toasted (see Tip, page 20)	1 cup	250 mL

Citrus Balsamic Vinaigrette: Combine all 4 ingredients in jar with tight-fitting lid. Shake well. Makes about 1/2 cup (125 mL) vinaigrette.

Salad: Put first 4 ingredients into large bowl. Toss. Drizzle with Citrus Balsamic Vinaigrette. Toss.

Sprinkle with walnuts. Makes about 8 cups (2 L). Serves 4.

1 serving: 267 Calories; 20.0 g Total Fat (2.7 g Mono, 14.3 g Poly, 1.9 g Sat); 0 mg Cholesterol; 19 g Carbohydrate; 6 g Fibre; 8 g Protein; 81 mg Sodium

Pictured on front cover.

Paré Pointer

At least when you make mistakes on a computer, you can put them in alphabetical order.

Herbed Potato Salad

A little bit of green makes this avocado and smoky bacon potato salad a unique picnic treat. A great partner for Crispy Chicken Drumettes, page 84, and roasted veggies.

FRESH HERB MAYONNAISE

Mayonnaise	1/3 cup	75 mL
Chopped fresh chives	2 tbsp.	30 mL
Chopped fresh mint	2 tbsp.	30 mL
Chopped fresh parsley	2 tbsp.	30 mL
Dijon mustard	2 tbsp.	30 mL
Salt	1/8 tsp.	0.5 mL
Pepper, sprinkle		

SALAD

Red potatoes, peeled and quartered	3 lbs.	1.4 kg
Bacon slices, cooked crisp and crumbled	4	4
Thinly sliced green onion	1/3 cup	75 mL
Ripe large avocado, chopped	1	1

Fresh Herb Mayonnaise: Combine all 7 ingredients in small bowl. Makes about 1/2 cup (125 mL) mayonnaise.

Salad: Cook potato in boiling salted water in large saucepan until just tender. Drain. Rinse with cold water. Drain well. Cut into 1 inch (2.5 cm) pieces. Put into large bowl.

Add bacon and green onion. Toss. Add Fresh Herb Mayonnaise. Toss.

Scatter avocado over top. Makes about 9 cups (2.25 L). Serves 6.

1 serving: 405 Calories; 21.5 g Total Fat (13.3 g Mono, 5.1 g Poly, 5.7 g Sat); 17 mg Cholesterol; 49 g Carbohydrate; 6 g Fibre; 6 g Protein; 276 mg Sodium

Pictured on page 72.

Vegetable Pearl Salad

Certainly a salad to treasure. Marinated artichokes give pearl barley a unique spin. Simply sensational with Dijon Dill Salmon Patties, page 106.

Water	1 1/2 cups	375 mL
Pearl barley	1/2 cup	125 mL
Salt	1/4 tsp.	1 mL
Diced red pepper	2 cups	500 mL
Quartered fresh white mushrooms	2 cups	500 mL
Jar of marinated artichokes, drained, marinade reserved, chopped	12 oz.	340 mL
Reserved artichoke marinade	1/2 cup	125 mL
Grated Parmesan cheese	2 tbsp.	30 mL
Lemon juice	1 tbsp.	15 mL
Garlic clove, minced (or 1/4 tsp., 1 mL, powder)	1	1
Italian seasoning	1 tsp.	5 mL
Granulated sugar	1 tsp.	5 mL
Salt	1/4 tsp.	1 mL
Pepper, sprinkle		

Chopped fresh basil, for garnish

Combine first 3 ingredients in small saucepan. Bring to a boil. Reduce heat to medium-low. Simmer, partially covered, for about 30 minutes until barley is tender. Drain. Rinse with cold water. Drain well. Transfer to large bowl.

Add next 3 ingredients. Toss.

Process next 8 ingredients in blender or food processor until smooth. Add to barley mixture. Toss.

Garnish with basil. Makes about 6 cups (1.5 L). Serves 6.

1 serving: 123 Calories; 5.1 g Total Fat (0.2 g Mono, 0.2 g Poly, 0.5 g Sat); 2 mg Cholesterol; 20 g Carbohydrate; 5 g Fibre; 3 g Protein; 701 mg Sodium

Rice Noodle Salad

Perfect when you want to experience the lighter side of things—thin noodles, crunchy veggies and mildly-spiced dressing. Pair with Zesty Chicken Kabobs, page 92.

PEANUT DRESSING

Peanut sauce	2/3 cup	150 mL
Soy sauce	2 1/2 tbsp.	37 mL
Chopped fresh cilantro or parsley (or 3/4 tsp., 4 mL, dried)	1 tbsp.	15 mL

SALAD

Rice vermicelli	9 oz.	255 g
Shredded bok choy, lightly packed	2 cups	500 mL
Diced red pepper	1 cup	250 mL
Can of sliced water chestnuts, drained and finely chopped	8 oz.	227 mL
Grated carrot	1/2 cup	125 mL
Chopped salted peanuts	1/2 cup	125 mL

Peanut Dressing: Combine all 3 ingredients in small bowl. Makes about 2/3 cup (150 mL) dressing.

Salad: Put vermicelli into large bowl. Cover with boiling water. Let stand for about 5 minutes until tender. Drain. Rinse with cold water. Drain well. Return to same bowl.

Add next 4 ingredients. Toss. Drizzle Peanut Dressing over salad. Toss.

Sprinkle with peanuts. Makes about 8 cups (2 L). Serves 4.

1 serving: 380 Calories; 7.3 g Total Fat (trace Mono, 0.1 g Poly, 1.5 g Sat); 0 mg Cholesterol; 65 g Carbohydrate; 4 g Fibre; 11 g Protein; 1574 mg Sodium

Pictured on page 90.

Minted Pea Salad

Fresh mint enhances a simple mix of green peas and chickpeas. Serve with Curry-Spiced Chicken, page 85, and basmati rice—and dinner will be in mint condition!

Frozen peas, thawed	3 cups	750 mL
Can of chickpeas (garbanzo beans), rinsed and drained	19 oz.	540 mL
Chopped fresh mint	3 tbsp.	50 mL
Finely chopped green onion	2 tbsp.	30 mL
SWEET LIME VINAIGRETTE		
Cooking oil	1/3 cup	75 mL
Red wine vinegar	3 tbsp.	50 mL
Granulated sugar	1 tbsp.	15 mL
Garlic clove, minced (or 1/4 tsp., 1 mL, powder)	1	1
Grated lime zest	1 tsp.	5 mL
Lime juice	1 tsp.	5 mL
Salt	1/2 tsp.	2 mL
Pepper	1/4 tsp.	1 mL

Put first 4 ingredients into large bowl. Toss.

Sweet Lime Vinaigrette: Combine all 8 ingredients in jar with tight-fitting lid. Shake well. Makes about 1/2 cup (125 mL) vinaigrette. Drizzle over salad. Toss. Makes about 5 3/4 cups (1.45 L). Serves 4.

1 serving: 472 Calories; 21.2 g Total Fat (11.0 g Mono, 6.9 g Poly, 1.7 g Sat); 0 mg Cholesterol; 56 g Carbohydrate; 11 g Fibre; 18 g Protein; 742 mg Sodium

1. Grilled Lamb Kabobs, page 121
2. Curry-Spiced Chicken, page 85
3. Minted Pea Salad, above
4. Cabbage Noodles, page 62

Props courtesy of: Pfaltzgraff Canada

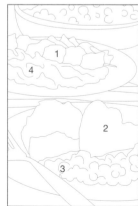

Dill Pasta Salad

Looking for the real dill? This super-easy macaroni salad fits the bill. A versatile side for any barbecue meal—especially Balsamic Skewers, page 99.

Elbow macaroni	1 1/2 cups	375 mL
Chopped tomato	3/4 cup	175 mL
Chopped celery	1/2 cup	125 mL
Grated Parmesan cheese	1/3 cup	75 mL
Chopped red (or green) onion	1/4 cup	60 mL
DRESSING		
Mayonnaise	1/2 cup	125 mL
Tangy dill relish	3 tbsp.	50 mL
Chopped fresh dill (or 3/4 tsp., 4 mL, dried)	1 tbsp.	15 mL
Prepared mustard	1 tsp.	5 mL

Cook macaroni in boiling salted water in large uncovered saucepan for 8 to 10 minutes, stirring occasionally, until tender but firm. Drain. Rinse with cold water. Drain well. Transfer to medium bowl.

Add next 4 ingredients. Toss.

Dressing: Combine all 4 ingredients in small bowl. Add to salad. Toss. Makes about 6 cups (1.5 L). Serves 4.

1 serving: 397 Calories; 25.3 g Total Fat (13.1 g Mono, 7.8 g Poly, 3.7 g Sat); 23 mg Cholesterol; 33 g Carbohydrate; 2 g Fibre; 9 g Protein; 434 mg Sodium

Pictured at left.

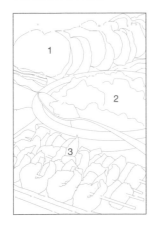

1. Cajun Cheese Bread, page 40
2. Dill Pasta Salad, above
3. Balsamic Skewers, page 99

Props courtesy of: Emile Henry

Apple Date Salad

Your first date with this salad will definitely lead to a second...and a third!
Serve this savoury and sweet beauty with roasted pork and stuffing.

BLUE CHEESE DRESSING

Mayonnaise	2 tbsp.	30 mL
Sour cream	2 tbsp.	30 mL
Crumbled blue cheese	1 1/2 tbsp.	25 mL
Apple cider vinegar	1 tbsp.	15 mL
Garlic powder	1/8 tsp.	0.5 mL

SALAD

Medium unpeeled cooking apples (such as McIntosh), diced (see Note)	2	2
Mixed salad greens, lightly packed	6 cups	1.5 L
Chopped pitted dates	1 cup	250 mL
Pecan halves, toasted (see Tip, below)	1/2 cup	125 mL

Blue Cheese Dressing: Combine all 5 ingredients in medium bowl. Makes about 6 tbsp. (100 mL) dressing.

Salad: Put apple into large bowl. Add Blue Cheese Dressing (see Note). Toss until coated.

Add salad greens. Toss.

Sprinkle with dates and pecans. Makes about 10 cups (2.5 L). Serves 8.

1 serving: 171 Calories; 8.9 g Total Fat (4.4 g Mono, 2.5 g Poly, 1.4 g Sat); 6 mg Cholesterol; 23 g Carbohydrate; 4 g Fibre; 2 g Protein; 52 mg Sodium

Note: Wait to dice the apple until just before assembling the salad. Adding dressing to apple as soon as it is cut helps to prevent browning.

 When toasting nuts, seeds or coconut, cooking times will vary for each different ingredient—so never toast them together. For small amounts, place ingredient in an ungreased shallow frying pan. Heat on medium for 3 to 5 minutes, stirring often, until golden. For larger amounts, spread ingredient evenly in an ungreased shallow pan. Bake in a 350°F (175°C) oven for 5 to 10 minutes, stirring or shaking often, until golden.

Potato And Green Bean Salad

There's nothing wrong with a little green. Potatoes and green beans are accented with subtle flavours of mint and mustard. A great addition to Cajun Cutlets, page 139.

Red baby potatoes, halved	2 lbs.	900 g
Fresh (or frozen) whole green beans, halved diagonally	1 lb.	454 g
Green onions, sliced diagonally	3	3
Slivered red pepper	1/4 cup	60 mL
MINT MUSTARD DRESSING		
Olive (or cooking) oil	1/4 cup	60 mL
Red wine vinegar	2 tbsp.	30 mL
Liquid honey	1 tbsp.	15 mL
Dijon mustard (with whole seeds)	1 tbsp.	15 mL
Lemon juice	1 tbsp.	15 mL
Finely chopped fresh mint	2 tsp.	10 mL
Salt	1 tsp.	5 mL
Lemon pepper, sprinkle		

Cook potato in boiling salted water in large covered saucepan for 5 minutes.

Add green beans. Reduce heat to medium-low. Simmer, covered, for 5 to 7 minutes until potato is tender and green beans are tender-crisp. Drain. Transfer to large bowl.

Add green onion and red pepper. Toss.

Mint Mustard Dressing: Combine all 8 ingredients in small bowl. Makes about 1/2 cup (125 mL) dressing. Let stand for 10 minutes to blend flavours. Drizzle over salad. Toss. Makes about 5 cups (1.25 L). Serves 4.

1 serving: 364 Calories; 13.7 g Total Fat (10.0 g Mono, 1.2 g Poly, 1.9 g Sat); 0 mg Cholesterol; 54 g Carbohydrate; 7 g Fibre; 8 g Protein; 656 mg Sodium

Jicama Salad

This is one heck of a jicama dish! Jicama (pronounced HEE-kah-mah) is a crunchy, slightly sweet root vegetable that's also fondly known as the Mexican potato. Combined with sweet raisins, almonds and a refreshing citrus vinaigrette, it provides a nice contrast to Polenta-Topped Chili, page 78.

Julienned peeled jicama (see Tip, page 140)	3 cups	750 mL
Medium orange, peeled and chopped	1	1
Chopped fresh parsley	1/2 cup	125 mL
Dark raisins	1/2 cup	125 mL
Sliced almonds, toasted (see Tip, page 20)	1/2 cup	125 mL
SPICY LIME VINAIGRETTE		
Cooking oil	1/4 cup	60 mL
Lime juice	1/4 cup	60 mL
Ground cumin	1/4 tsp.	1 mL
Salt	1/4 tsp.	1 mL
Chili paste (sambal oelek)	1/4 tsp.	1 mL

Put first 5 ingredients into medium bowl. Toss.

Spicy Lime Vinaigrette: Combine all 5 ingredients in jar with tight-fitting lid. Shake well. Makes about 1/2 cup (125 mL) vinaigrette. Drizzle over salad. Toss. Makes about 4 1/2 cups (1.1 L). Serves 6.

1 serving: 207 Calories; 13.3 g Total Fat (7.9 g Mono, 3.7 g Poly, 1.0 g Sat); 0 mg Cholesterol; 22 g Carbohydrate; 5 g Fibre; 3 g Protein; 105 mg Sodium

Pictured on page 53.

Paré Pointer
The prettiest figure in geometry is acute angle.

Pecan Potato Salad

Wow them at the next get together with this highly unusual and superbly stylish potato salad. You're not going to find this one at the deli! Outstanding with Goat Cheese Crostini, page 58, and grilled salmon.

Thinly sliced English cucumber (with peel)	3 cups	750 mL
Cut or torn romaine lettuce, lightly packed	3 cups	750 mL
Can of sweet potatoes, drained and chopped	19 oz.	540 mL
Thinly sliced celery	2 cups	500 mL
Thinly sliced red onion	2/3 cup	150 mL
Coarsely chopped pecans, toasted (see Tip, page 20)	2/3 cup	150 mL
Shaved Asiago (or Parmesan) cheese	1/2 cup	125 mL
TOMATO DRESSING		
Tomato juice	1/2 cup	125 mL
Olive (or cooking) oil	1/4 cup	60 mL
Chopped fresh basil (or 1 1/2 tsp., 7 mL, dried)	2 tbsp.	30 mL
Granulated sugar	2 tsp.	10 mL
Salt	1/2 tsp.	2 mL

Put first 7 ingredients into large bowl. Toss.

Tomato Dressing: Combine all 5 ingredients in jar with tight-fitting lid. Shake well. Makes about 1 cup (250 mL) dressing. Drizzle over salad. Toss. Makes about 12 cups (3 L). Serves 6.

1 serving: 333 Calories; 21.5 g Total Fat (11.8 g Mono, 3.7 g Poly, 3.8 g Sat); 8 mg Cholesterol; 33 g Carbohydrate; 6 g Fibre; 6 g Protein; 429 mg Sodium

Pictured on page 36 and on back cover.

Grilled Beef Tomato Salad

Reach for some Asian-inspired ginger sesame dressing to add a touch of the exotic to this fresh yet hearty steak and tomato meal.

Sesame ginger dressing	3 tbsp.	50 mL
Garlic cloves, minced (or 1/2 tsp., 2 mL, powder)	2	2
Red curry paste	1/2 tsp.	2 mL
Flank steak	1 lb.	454 g
Medium tomatoes, each cut into 8 wedges	3	3
Green onions, sliced	4	4
Sesame ginger dressing	3 tbsp.	50 mL
Chopped fresh cilantro or parsley	2 tbsp.	30 mL
Chopped fresh mint	2 tbsp.	30 mL
Lime juice	2 tbsp.	30 mL
Fresh, thin Chinese-style egg noodles, cut in half	8 oz.	225 g
Sesame ginger dressing	1/3 cup	75 mL
Cut or torn green leaf lettuce, lightly packed	6 cups	1.5 L

Combine first 3 ingredients in small cup.

Brush dressing mixture on both sides of beef. Let stand for 30 minutes. Preheat gas barbecue to medium (see Tip, page 56). Cook beef on greased grill for about 4 minutes per side for medium-rare or until desired doneness. Remove to cutting board. Let stand for 5 minutes. Thinly slice beef diagonally. Put into large bowl.

Add next 6 ingredients. Toss. Set aside.

Cook noodles in boiling salted water in large uncovered saucepan or Dutch oven for about 3 minutes, stirring occasionally, until tender but firm. Drain. Rinse with cold water. Drain well. Transfer to medium bowl.

Drizzle second amount of dressing over noodles. Toss.

Arrange lettuce on 4 large plates. Top with noodles and beef mixture. Serves 4.

1 serving: 611 Calories; 27.6 g Total Fat (3.7 g Mono, 1.2 g Poly, 8.5 g Sat); 103 mg Cholesterol; 59 g Carbohydrate; 6 g Fibre; 37 g Protein; 477 mg Sodium

Pictured on page 90.

Chicken Couscous Salad

Couscous takes an Asian spin in this sweet, tangy,
citrusy salad. Best served at room temperature.

Prepared chicken broth	3 cups	750 mL
Box of plain couscous	12 oz.	340 g
Broccoli slaw	4 cups	1 L
(or shredded cabbage with carrot)		
Chopped cooked chicken	2 cups	500 mL
Can of mandarin orange segments, drained	10 oz.	284 mL
Thinly sliced red onion	1/2 cup	125 mL

ORANGE GINGER DRESSING

Orange juice	6 tbsp.	100 mL
Lemon juice	1/4 cup	60 mL
Olive (or cooking) oil	1/4 cup	60 mL
Finely grated gingerroot (or 3/4 tsp.,	1 tbsp.	15 mL
4 mL, ground ginger)		
Grated orange zest	2 tsp.	10 mL
Garlic cloves, minced (or 1/2 tsp.,	2	2
2 mL, powder)		
Dried crushed chilies	1/4 tsp.	1 mL
Salt	1/4 tsp.	1 mL

Measure broth into medium saucepan. Bring to a boil. Add couscous. Stir. Remove from heat. Let stand, covered, for about 5 minutes until couscous is tender and broth is absorbed. Fluff with a fork. Transfer to large bowl. Cool.

Add next 4 ingredients. Toss.

Orange Ginger Dressing: Combine all 8 ingredients in jar with tight-fitting lid. Shake well. Makes about 1 cup (250 mL) dressing. Drizzle over salad. Toss. Let stand for 15 minutes to blend flavours. Makes about 13 cups (3.25 L). Serves 6.

1 serving: 443 Calories; 13.3 g Total Fat (8.2 g Mono, 1.8 g Poly, 2.4 g Sat); 35 mg Cholesterol; 57 g Carbohydrate; 4 g Fibre; 23 g Protein; 554 mg Sodium

Sunny Rice Salad

This cheerful, yellow salad with mango dressing will brighten everyone's day! Serve on a bed of mixed salad greens for a complete meal.

TANGY MANGO DRESSING		
Finely chopped mango chutney	2 tbsp.	30 mL
Water	1 tbsp.	15 mL
Apple cider vinegar	2 tsp.	10 mL
Ketchup	1 tsp.	5 mL
Cooking oil	1 tsp.	5 mL
Salt, sprinkle		
Pepper, sprinkle		

SALAD		
Cooked long grain white rice (about 1 cup, 250 mL, uncooked)	3 cups	750 mL
Salad dressing (or mayonnaise)	1/2 cup	125 mL
Turmeric	1/4 tsp.	1 mL
Deli ham, cut into 1/8 inch (3 mm) strips (or 6 1/2 oz., 184 g, can of flaked ham, drained and crumbled)	6 oz.	170 g
Large hard-cooked eggs, quartered lengthwise (or sliced)	6	6
Chopped fresh parsley	2 tbsp.	30 mL

Tangy Mango Dressing: Combine all 7 ingredients in small bowl. Makes about 1/4 cup (60 mL) dressing.

Salad: Combine first 3 ingredients in medium bowl. Spread on large serving plate.

Scatter ham over rice mixture. Arrange egg on top. Drizzle Tangy Mango Dressing over salad.

Sprinkle with parsley. Makes about 5 1/2 cups. Serves 6.

1 serving: 360 Calories; 22.2 g Total Fat (10.8 g Mono, 5.9 g Poly, 3.4 g Sat); 236 mg Cholesterol; 26 g Carbohydrate; trace Fibre; 14 g Protein; 541 mg Sodium

Grilled Pork And Mango Salad

Hickory, dickory, dock...it's almost six o' clock! Do you know what you're making for dinner? This is it—refreshing, sweet mango and grilled pork tenderloin. Tastes even better with Sun-Dried Tomato Cornbread, page 50.

Pork tenderloin, trimmed of fat	1 lb.	454 g
Chili powder	1 tsp.	5 mL
Hickory barbecue sauce	1/4 cup	60 mL
Cut or torn romaine lettuce, lightly packed	8 cups	2 L
Can of sliced mango in syrup, drained and chopped	14 oz.	398 mL
Thinly sliced red pepper	1 cup	250 mL
SWEET 'N' SPICY DRESSING		
Italian (or ranch) dressing	1/2 cup	125 mL
Lime (or orange) juice	2 tbsp.	30 mL
Liquid honey	2 tbsp.	30 mL
Chili powder	1/2 tsp.	2 mL

Sprinkle all sides of tenderloin with chili powder. Preheat gas barbecue to medium. Place tenderloin on 1 side of greased grill. Turn off burner under tenderloin, leaving opposite burner on medium. Close lid. Cook for 25 minutes, turning occasionally.

Brush tenderloin with barbecue sauce. Cook for another 4 to 5 minutes until meat thermometer inserted into thickest part of tenderloin reads 155°F (68°C). Remove to cutting board. Cover with foil. Let stand for 10 minutes. Cut into 12 slices.

Layer next 3 ingredients on 4 large plates. Top with pork.

Sweet 'N' Spicy Dressing: Combine all 4 ingredients in small bowl. Makes about 3/4 cup (175 mL) dressing. Drizzle over salads. Serves 4.

1 serving: 474 Calories; 23.9 g Total Fat (12.7 g Mono, 7.4 g Poly, 2.6 g Sat); 87 mg Cholesterol; 38 g Carbohydrate; 4 g Fibre; 30 g Protein; 702 mg Sodium

Pictured on page 53.

Tex-Mex Toss

Toss on your sombrero and toss up some fun with this fresh and easy salad!

Cut or torn romaine lettuce, lightly packed	8 cups	2 L
Chopped cooked chicken	3 cups	750 mL
Can of black beans, rinsed and drained	19 oz.	540 mL
Diced medium Cheddar cheese	1 cup	250 mL
Halved cherry tomatoes	1 cup	250 mL
Ranch dressing	2/3 cup	150 mL
Can of sliced black olives	4 1/2 oz.	125 mL
Salsa	1/3 cup	75 mL
Chopped avocado	2 cups	500 mL
Lemon juice	2 tsp.	10 mL
Coarsely crushed nacho chips	2 cups	500 mL

Put first 8 ingredients into extra-large bowl. Toss.

Put avocado into small bowl. Sprinkle with lemon juice. Toss until coated. Scatter over salad.

Sprinkle with chips. Makes about 16 cups (4 L). Serves 6.

1 serving: 660 Calories; 39.5 g Total Fat (13.2 g Mono, 3.4 g Poly, 9.8 g Sat); 80 mg Cholesterol; 45 g Carbohydrate; 13 g Fibre; 35 g Protein; 1016 mg Sodium

Chicken Pita Salad

A super supper salad everyone will enjoy. Light fare for a late evening meal.

Chopped cooked chicken	3 cups	750 mL
Chopped tomato	1 1/2 cups	375 mL
Chopped English cucumber (with peel)	1 1/2 cups	375 mL
Italian dressing	2/3 cup	150 mL
Chopped radish	1/2 cup	125 mL
Chopped fresh parsley	1/3 cup	75 mL
Lemon juice	2 tbsp.	30 mL
Pita bread (7 inch, 18 cm, diameter)	2	2
Italian dressing	1 tbsp.	15 mL

(continued on next page)

Combine first 7 ingredients in large bowl. Let stand for 10 minutes to blend flavours.

Put pitas on greased baking sheet. Brush with second amount of dressing. Bake in 375°F (190°C) oven for about 6 minutes per side until crisp. Break into irregular 1 to 1 1/2 inch (2.5 to 3.8 cm) pieces. Add to salad. Toss. Makes about 8 cups (2 L). Serves 4.

1 serving: 537 Calories; 35.8 g Total Fat (18.4 g Mono, 11.3 g Poly, 4.0 g Sat); 106 mg Cholesterol; 24 g Carbohydrate; 2 g Fibre; 30 g Protein; 897 mg Sodium

Peanut Noodle Salad

Say nuts to turning on the stove on a hot summer day.
Just the thing when it's too hot to cook.

Rice vermicelli	9 oz.	255 g
Smooth peanut butter	1/3 cup	75 mL
Brown sugar, packed	1/4 cup	60 mL
Lemon juice	1/4 cup	60 mL
Soy sauce	2 tbsp.	30 mL
Hot water	2 tbsp.	30 mL
Chopped cooked chicken	2 cups	500 mL
Thinly sliced red pepper	2 cups	500 mL
Grated carrot	1 cup	250 mL
Sliced green onion	1/2 cup	125 mL
Heads of butter lettuce, leaves separated	2	2

Put vermicelli into large bowl. Cover with boiling water. Let stand for about 5 minutes until tender. Drain. Rinse with cold water. Drain well. Return to same bowl.

Combine next 5 ingredients in small bowl. Add to vermicelli. Toss until coated.

Add next 4 ingredients. Toss.

Arrange lettuce on 4 large plates. Top with vermicelli mixture. Serves 4.

1 serving: 456 Calories; 5.1 g Total Fat (1.8 g Mono, 1.3 g Poly, 1.4 g Sat); 53 mg Cholesterol; 73 g Carbohydrate; 4 g Fibre; 25 g Protein; 742 mg Sodium

Pork And Pasta Salad

Pork, pasta and peppers, punctuated with a pleasantly creamy buttermilk dressing. Serve at room temperature or chilled with fresh sourdough bread. Cook extra pasta tonight to make light work of this recipe tomorrow.

Olive (or cooking) oil	2 tsp.	10 mL
Pork tenderloin, trimmed of fat and cut into thin strips	3/4 lb.	340 g
Bacon slices, diced	2	2
Pepper, sprinkle		
Sliced fresh white mushrooms	1 1/2 cups	375 mL
Thinly sliced green pepper	1 cup	250 mL
Thinly sliced red pepper	1 cup	250 mL
Cooked medium bow (or other) pasta (about 2 1/4 cups, 550 mL, uncooked)	3 cups	750 mL
BUTTERMILK DRESSING		
Buttermilk	1/3 cup	75 mL
Olive (or cooking) oil	2 tbsp.	30 mL
Red wine vinegar	1 tbsp.	15 mL
Dijon mustard	1 tbsp.	15 mL
Liquid honey	1 tbsp.	15 mL
Chopped fresh oregano (or 3/4 tsp., 4 mL, dried)	1 tbsp.	15 mL

Heat olive oil in large frying pan on medium-high. Add next 3 ingredients. Cook for about 5 minutes, stirring occasionally, until pork is browned.

Add next 3 ingredients. Stir. Cook for about 5 minutes, stirring occasionally, until peppers are tender-crisp. Transfer to large bowl.

Add pasta. Toss.

Buttermilk Dressing: Process all 6 ingredients in blender or food processor until smooth. Makes about 2/3 cup (150 mL) dressing. Drizzle over salad. Toss. Chill. Makes about 8 cups (2 L). Serves 4.

1 serving: 345 Calories; 13.5 g Total Fat (8.3 g Mono, 1.6 g Poly, 2.7 g Sat); 54 mg Cholesterol; 29 g Carbohydrate; 2 g Fibre; 27 g Protein; 189 mg Sodium

Asian Salsa Salad

*Are we blending two cultures' cuisines? Absolutely! It's fusion
at its finest. Why not have the best of both worlds—in one dish.
If you're not a fan of tofu, this salad is sure to make you one.*

Chopped tomato	3 cups	750 mL
English cucumber (with peel), seeds removed, diced	1 cup	250 mL
Chopped red onion	1 cup	250 mL
Chopped fresh cilantro or parsley	1/4 cup	60 mL
Rice vinegar	1/4 cup	60 mL
Lime juice	3 tbsp.	50 mL
Sesame (or cooking) oil	1 tbsp.	15 mL
Granulated sugar	1 tbsp.	15 mL
Grated lime zest	1 tsp.	5 mL
Salt	1/2 tsp.	2 mL
Cooked long grain white rice (about 2/3 cup, 150 mL, uncooked)	2 cups	500 mL
Package of firm tofu, cut into 1/2 inch (12 mm) cubes	12 1/2 oz.	350 g
Chopped or torn romaine lettuce, lightly packed	6 cups	1.5 L

Combine first 10 ingredients in large bowl.

Add rice and tofu. Stir gently. Let stand for 30 minutes to blend flavours.

Arrange lettuce on 4 large plates. Top with tofu mixture. Serves 4.

*1 serving: 260 Calories; 6.5 g Total Fat (2.0 g Mono, 3.1 g Poly, 1.0 g Sat); 0 mg Cholesterol;
41 g Carbohydrate; 4 g Fibre; 11 g Protein; 343 mg Sodium*

Paré Pointer
Huge ships don't sink very often. Only once.

Maple Miso Tofu Salad

Thought miso was only for soup? Think again, this Japanese treat is just as tasty in a salad—especially when it's maple-glazed and served on a colourful bed of vegetables and noodles. Use whichever miso you prefer—the darker it is, the stronger its flavour.

Package of firm tofu	12 1/2 oz.	350 g
Maple (or maple-flavoured) syrup	1/3 cup	75 mL
Miso (see Note)	3 tbsp.	50 mL
Cayenne pepper, sprinkle		
Mixed salad greens, lightly packed	8 cups	2 L
Thinly sliced red pepper	2 cups	500 mL
Dry chow mein noodles	2 cups	500 mL
MAPLE SYRUP VINAIGRETTE		
Cooking oil	2 tbsp.	30 mL
Rice vinegar	1 tbsp.	15 mL
Maple (or maple-flavoured) syrup	1 tbsp.	15 mL
Sesame oil	1 tsp.	5 mL
Soy sauce	1 tsp.	5 mL

Cut tofu crosswise into 8 slices. Let stand on paper towels for about 5 minutes to drain. Arrange tofu on greased foil-lined baking sheet with sides.

Combine next 3 ingredients in small bowl. Brush on tofu. Broil on top rack in oven for about 3 minutes until edges are golden. Turn tofu over. Brush with remaining syrup mixture. Broil for another 3 to 5 minutes until edges are golden.

Put next 3 ingredients into large bowl. Toss.

Maple Syrup Vinaigrette: Combine all 5 ingredients in jar with tight-fitting lid. Shake well. Makes about 1/4 cup (60 mL) vinaigrette. Drizzle over salad. Toss. Arrange on 4 large plates. Top with tofu. Serves 4.

1 serving: 331 Calories; 11.8 g Total Fat (5.1 g Mono, 4.5 g Poly, 1.2 g Sat); 2 mg Cholesterol; 46 g Carbohydrate; 5 g Fibre; 13 g Protein; 700 mg Sodium

Pictured on page 90.

Note: Miso is fermented soy bean paste. It is available in specialty Asian grocery stores.

Spinach Chicken Salad

*It just makes sense that chicken and chickpeas would go together
so well—especially in a feta-studded salad. Serve with garlic toast.
Freeze leftover chickpeas in a small resealable freezer bag
to use another day in a salad, soup or stew.*

Fresh spinach leaves, lightly packed	4 cups	1 L
Canned chickpeas (garbanzo beans), rinsed and drained	1 cup	250 mL
Crumbled feta cheese	1/4 cup	60 mL
Cooking oil	2 tsp.	10 mL
Boneless, skinless chicken breast halves, chopped	3/4 lb.	340 g
Cherry tomatoes	16	16
LEMON OREGANO VINAIGRETTE		
Lemon juice	3 tbsp.	50 mL
Olive (or cooking) oil	4 tsp.	20 mL
Liquid honey	1 tbsp.	15 mL
Dried whole oregano	1 tsp.	5 mL
Ground cumin	1/2 tsp.	2 mL

Put first 3 ingredients into large bowl. Toss. Set aside.

Heat cooking oil in large frying pan on medium-high. Add chicken. Cook
for about 5 minutes, stirring often, until no longer pink inside.

Add tomatoes. Heat and stir on medium for about 5 minutes until
tomatoes are softened. Add to spinach mixture. Toss.

Lemon Oregano Vinaigrette: Combine all 5 ingredients in jar with
tight-fitting lid. Shake well. Makes about 1/3 cup (75 mL) vinaigrette.
Drizzle over salad. Toss. Makes about 8 cups (2 L). Serves 4.

*1 serving: 292 Calories; 11.7 g Total Fat (5.7 g Mono, 2.1 g Poly, 2.8 g Sat); 58 mg Cholesterol;
21 g Carbohydrate; 4 g Fibre; 27 g Protein; 303 mg Sodium*

Pesto Bean Salad

Ciabatta up! Consider all your bases loaded—with bread,
beans and cheese. This is a guaranteed home run!

Cubed ciabatta bread, toasted (see Note)	3 cups	750 mL
Can of red kidney beans, rinsed and drained	19 oz.	540 mL
Chopped tomato	2 cups	500 mL
Diced mozzarella cheese (see Note)	1 cup	250 mL
Thinly sliced red onion	1/2 cup	125 mL
Pine nuts, toasted (see Tip, page 20)	1/4 cup	60 mL
Basil pesto	1/4 cup	60 mL
Italian dressing	1/4 cup	60 mL
Cut or torn romaine lettuce, lightly packed	5 cups	1.25 L

Put first 6 ingredients into large bowl. Toss.

Combine pesto and dressing in small bowl. Add to bread mixture. Toss.

Arrange lettuce on 4 large plates. Top with bean mixture. Serves 4.

1 serving: 624 Calories; 30.1 g Total Fat (9.5 g Mono, 5.9 g Poly, 6.9 g Sat); 37 mg Cholesterol; 64 g Carbohydrate; 17 g Fibre; 26 g Protein; 745 mg Sodium

Pictured at right.

Note: To easily toast bread cubes, spread on an ungreased baking sheet with sides. Bake in a 350°F (175°C) oven for 10 to 12 minutes, tossing once at halftime.

Note: For easier dicing, chill mozzarella cheese in the freezer for 30 minutes.

1. Pesto Bean Salad, above
2. Sicilian Summer Grill, page 82

Props courtesy of: Casa Bugatti

Seafood Spinach Salad

A salad with a healthy helping of two of the sea's best offerings—shrimp and crab. Add Goat Cheese Crostini, page 58, and dinner's complete.

Fresh spinach leaves, lightly packed	7 cups	1.75 L
Cooked salad shrimp	12 oz.	340 g
Grated carrot	1/2 cup	125 mL
Slivered red pepper	1/2 cup	125 mL
Can of crabmeat, drained, cartilage removed, flaked	4 1/4 oz.	120 g
Green onions, sliced	2	2
DILL DRESSING		
Salad dressing (or mayonnaise)	1/2 cup	125 mL
Milk	2 tbsp.	30 mL
Chopped fresh dill (or 1/2 tsp., 2 mL, dried)	2 tsp.	10 mL
Lemon juice	1 tsp.	5 mL
Granulated sugar	3/4 tsp.	4 mL

Put first 6 ingredients into extra-large bowl. Toss.

Dill Dressing: Combine all 5 ingredients in small bowl. Makes about 1/2 cup (125 mL) dressing. Drizzle over salad. Toss. Makes about 8 cups (2 L). Serves 4.

1 serving: 394 Calories; 30.8 g Total Fat (14.4 g Mono, 11.5 g Poly, 3.4 g Sat); 113 mg Cholesterol; 10 g Carbohydrate; 4 g Fibre; 21 g Protein; 630 mg Sodium

Pictured at left and on back cover.

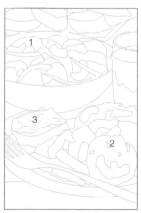

1. Pecan Potato Salad, page 23
2. Seafood Spinach Salad, above
3. Sun-Dried Tomato Crostini, page 59

Props courtesy of: Totally Bamboo

Roasted Garlic Pesto Muffins

Looking for a good side dish? Ever consider muffins? These savoury quick breads were made for mopping up the best part of saucy dishes like chilies or stews. Leave the garlic and onion in their skins for roasting.

Small garlic bulb	1	1
Small onion	1	1
All-purpose flour	2 cups	500 mL
Grated Parmesan cheese	1/4 cup	60 mL
Baking powder	1 tsp.	5 mL
Baking soda	1/2 tsp.	2 mL
Salt	1/2 tsp.	2 mL
Large eggs, fork-beaten	2	2
Buttermilk (or soured milk, see Note)	3/4 cup	175 mL
Butter (or hard margarine), melted	1/4 cup	60 mL
Basil pesto	2 tbsp.	30 mL
Liquid honey	2 tbsp.	30 mL

Trim 1/4 inch (6 mm) from garlic bulb to expose tops of cloves, leaving bulb intact. Trim 1/4 inch (6 mm) from top of onion. Wrap each in greased foil. Bake in 375°F (190°C) oven for about 45 minutes until tender. Let stand until cool enough to handle. Squeeze garlic bulb to remove cloves from skin. Discard skin. Put into medium bowl. Mash with a fork. Discard skin from onion. Chop onion. Add to garlic. Stir. Set aside.

Measure next 5 ingredients into large bowl. Stir. Make a well in centre.

Add remaining 5 ingredients to garlic mixture. Stir. Add to well. Stir until just moistened. Fill 12 greased muffin cups 2/3 full. Bake in 375°F (190°C) oven for about 15 minutes until wooden pick inserted in centre of muffin comes out clean. Let stand in pan for 5 minutes. Remove muffins and place on wire racks to cool. Makes 12 muffins.

1 muffin: 170 Calories; 6.9 g Total Fat (1.6 g Mono, 0.4 g Poly, 3.4 g Sat); 44 mg Cholesterol; 22 g Carbohydrate; 1 g Fibre; 5 g Protein; 287 mg Sodium

Pictured on page 144.

Note: To make soured milk, measure 2 tsp. (10 mL) white vinegar or lemon juice into a 1 cup (250 mL) liquid measure. Add enough milk to make 3/4 cup (175 mL). Stir. Let stand for 1 minute.

Oven-Roasted Ratatouille

This versatile dish is inordinately dee-lish. You can't go wrong with tender roasted veggies in a tangy tomato sauce with a hint of orange. Great topping pasta and complementing grilled chicken, pork or beef.

Medium zucchini (with peel), halved lengthwise and cut into 1/2 inch (12 mm) slices	1	1
Medium Asian eggplant (with peel), halved lengthwise and cut into 1/2 inch (12 mm) slices	1	1
Medium red peppers, cut into 1 inch (2.5 cm) pieces	2	2
Medium red onion, coarsely chopped	1	1
Sprigs of fresh rosemary	2	2
Strips of orange peel (2 inches, 5 cm, length, each)	2	2
Garlic cloves, coarsely chopped	3	3
Olive (or cooking) oil	2 tbsp.	30 mL
Tomato sauce	1 cup	250 mL
Salt	1/2 tsp.	2 mL
Pepper	1/4 tsp.	1 mL
Medium tomatoes, chopped	2	2
Chopped fresh basil	1/4 cup	60 mL
Orange juice	2 tbsp.	30 mL

Combine first 7 ingredients in ungreased 9 x 13 inch (22 x 33 cm) baking dish.

Drizzle with olive oil. Toss. Bake, uncovered, in 425°F (220°C) oven for 20 to 25 minutes, stirring occasionally, until vegetables start to soften.

Add next 3 ingredients. Stir. Bake, uncovered, for another 8 to 10 minutes until vegetables are softened. Discard rosemary sprigs and orange peel.

Add remaining 3 ingredients. Stir. Makes about 5 1/2 cups (1.4 L). Serves 6.

1 serving: 97 Calories; 4.9 g Total Fat (3.4 g Mono, 0.6 g Poly, 0.7 g Sat); 0 mg Cholesterol; 13 g Carbohydrate; 3 g Fibre; 2 g Protein; 449 mg Sodium

Cajun Cheese Bread

Topped with spicy jalapeño cheese and Cajun seasoning, this kicky French bread has gone French quarter! Excellent with Balsamic Skewers, page 99.

Butter (or hard margarine), softened	2/3 cup	150 mL
Grated jalapeño Monterey Jack cheese	2/3 cup	150 mL
Cajun seasoning	1 tsp.	5 mL
Parsley flakes	1/2 tsp.	2 mL
French bread loaf, cut into 12 slices	1	1

Combine first 4 ingredients in small bowl.

Spread cheese mixture on 1 side of bread slices. Arrange slices into loaf. Wrap tightly in sheet of heavy-duty (or double layer of regular) foil. Bake in 375°F (190°C) oven for 15 to 20 minutes, until cheese is melted. Makes 12 slices.

1 slice: 203 Calories; 12.5 g Total Fat (3.4 g Mono, 0.7 g Poly, 7.4 g Sat); 31 mg Cholesterol; 18 g Carbohydrate; 1 g Fibre; 5 g Protein; 358 mg Sodium

Pictured on page 18.

GRILLED CAJUN CHEESE BREAD: Preheat gas barbecue to medium. Place foil-wrapped loaf on ungreased grill. Close lid. Cook for about 15 minutes, turning occasionally, until cheese is melted.

Asiago Polenta

This Italian, cornmeal staple is rich and creamy with a hint of nutmeg. A tasty side for Sausage Pepper Skillet, page 142.

Prepared chicken broth	2 cups	500 mL
Water	2 cups	500 mL
Butter (or hard margarine)	2 tbsp.	30 mL
Salt	1/2 tsp.	2 mL
Ground nutmeg	1/4 tsp.	1 mL
Yellow cornmeal	1 cup	250 mL
Grated Asiago cheese	1 cup	250 mL

Combine first 5 ingredients in large saucepan. Bring to a boil.

(continued on next page)

Slowly add cornmeal, stirring constantly. Reduce heat to medium-low. Simmer, covered, for about 5 minutes, stirring often, until thickened.

Add cheese. Stir until melted. Makes about 4 cups (1 L). Serves 4.

1 serving: 307 Calories; 16.0 g Total Fat (1.9 g Mono, 0.6 g Poly, 8.9 g Sat); 40 mg Cholesterol; 28 g Carbohydrate; 2 g Fibre; 11 g Protein; 937 mg Sodium

Pictured on page 143.

Bulgur Vegetables

As an up-and-coming popular grain, bulgur is sure to please the health-conscious when mixed with citrus and fresh herbs. Excellent with Curry-Spiced Chicken, page 85, for a protein-packed meal. Add the leftover chickpeas to a chili or stew.

Boiling water	1 1/4 cups	300 mL
Bulgur, fine grind	3/4 cup	175 mL
Salt	1/2 tsp.	2 mL
Canned chickpeas (garbanzo beans), rinsed and drained	1 cup	250 mL
Frozen peas, thawed	1 cup	250 mL
Diced zucchini (with peel)	1 cup	250 mL
Diced red pepper	1/2 cup	125 mL
Italian dressing	1/3 cup	75 mL
Chopped fresh mint	2 tbsp.	30 mL
Chopped fresh basil	2 tbsp.	30 mL
Chopped fresh parsley	2 tbsp.	30 mL
Grated lemon zest	1 1/2 tsp.	7 mL

Combine first 3 ingredients in medium bowl. Let stand for about 20 minutes until water is absorbed. Fluff with a fork.

Combine next 8 ingredients in large bowl. Add bulgur. Toss.

Sprinkle with lemon zest. Makes about 5 cups (1.25 L). Serves 4.

1 serving: 311 Calories; 14.5 g Total Fat (7.4 g Mono, 5.0 g Poly, 1.1 g Sat); 12.5 mg Cholesterol; 39 g Carbohydrate; 7 g Fibre; 9 g Protein; 735 mg Sodium

Corn-Stuffed Tomatoes

Although there's a lot of corn in it, there's nothing corny about it
—a mild, cheesy filling is just the thing in a ripe, juicy tomato.
A sensational side for Chicken Tortilla Bake, page 95.

Large tomatoes	6	6
Salt, sprinkle		
Chopped onion	1 cup	250 mL
Can of kernel corn, drained	12 oz.	341 mL
Medium salsa	1/4 cup	60 mL
Light vegetable cream cheese	2 tbsp.	30 mL
Grated medium Cheddar cheese	1/4 cup	60 mL
Grated medium Cheddar cheese	1/4 cup	60 mL

Slice 1/4 inch (6 mm) from top of tomatoes. Scoop pulp into small bowl, leaving 1/4 inch (6 mm) thick shells (see Note). Trim bottom of tomatoes to sit flat, being careful not to cut into shells.

Sprinkle inside of tomatoes with salt. Let stand, cut-side down, on paper towels to drain.

Put onion into medium microwave-safe bowl. Microwave on high (100%) for about 2 minutes until softened.

Add next 3 ingredients. Stir until cream cheese is melted.

Add first amount of Cheddar cheese. Stir. Spoon into tomatoes. Arrange in greased 9 × 9 inch (22 × 22 cm) pan.

Sprinkle with second amount of Cheddar cheese. Broil on top rack in oven for about 3 minutes until Cheddar cheese is golden. Serves 6.

1 serving: 141 Calories; 4.8 g Total Fat (1.1 g Mono, 0.6 g Poly, 2.7 g Sat); 13 mg Cholesterol; 21 g Carbohydrate; 4 g Fibre; 6 g Protein; 258 mg Sodium

Note: The tomato pulp is too good to waste—use it in a tomato-based soup or stew.

Fresh Herb Rice

Fresh herbs, a hint of garlic and a lively splash of lemon make ordinary rice
fabulously fragrant and flavourful. Excellent with Feta Shrimp Frittata,
page 100, and steamed sugar snap peas. If you don't have
any cilantro on hand, simply double the parsley.

Butter (or hard margarine)	2 tbsp.	30 mL
Chopped onion	1/2 cup	125 mL
Garlic clove, minced (or 1/4 tsp., 1 mL, powder)	1	1
Long grain white rice	1 1/2 cups	375 mL
Water	2 1/2 cups	625 mL
Dry (or alcohol-free) white wine	1/4 cup	60 mL
Salt	1/2 tsp.	2 mL
Chopped fresh cilantro	2 tbsp.	30 mL
Chopped fresh parsley	2 tbsp.	30 mL
Chopped fresh dill	2 tbsp.	30 mL
Finely chopped green onion	2 tbsp.	30 mL
Grated lemon zest	1 tsp.	5 mL

Melt butter in medium saucepan on medium. Add onion and garlic. Cook for about 5 minutes, stirring often, until onion is softened.

Add rice. Stir until coated.

Add next 3 ingredients. Stir. Bring to a boil. Reduce heat to medium-low. Simmer, covered, for about 20 minutes, without stirring, until rice is tender and liquid is absorbed. Let stand for 5 minutes.

Add remaining 5 ingredients. Stir. Makes about 5 cups (1.25 L). Serves 4.

*1 serving: 328 Calories; 6.2 g Total Fat (1.6 g Mono, 0.4 g Poly, 3.7 g Sat); 15 mg Cholesterol;
59 g Carbohydrate; 1 g Fibre; 5 g Protein; 341 mg Sodium*

Orange Basil Broccoli

Nobody said broccoli had to be boring! Serve this yummy side with Bruschetta Steak Loaf, page 67.

Broccoli florets	6 cups	1.5 L
Sliced natural almonds, toasted (see Tip, page 20)	3 tbsp.	50 mL
Chopped fresh basil (or 3/4 tsp., 4 mL, dried)	1 tbsp.	15 mL
Salt, sprinkle		
Pepper, sprinkle		
Butter (or hard margarine), melted	2 tbsp.	30 mL
Frozen concentrated orange juice, thawed	2 tbsp.	30 mL

Put broccoli into greased 2 quart (2 L) casserole. Sprinkle with next 4 ingredients.

Combine butter and concentrated orange juice in small cup. Drizzle over broccoli. Cook, covered, in 375°F (190°C) oven for 20 to 30 minutes until broccoli is tender-crisp. Serves 4.

1 serving: 121 Calories; 8.3 g Total Fat (2.9 g Mono, 0.9 g Poly, 3.8 g Sat); 15 mg Cholesterol; 10 g Carbohydrate; 4 g Fibre; 4 g Protein; 69 mg Sodium

Pesto Potato Wedges

With a hint of basil pesto, these hearty home-fries are hardly French—maybe Italian. A great accompaniment for grilled steak or chicken and your favourite vegetables or salad.

Olive (or cooking) oil	1 tbsp.	15 mL
Seasoned salt	1/2 tsp.	2 mL
Pepper	1/8 tsp.	0.5 mL
Large unpeeled red potatoes, each cut into 8 wedges	4	4
Basil pesto	1/4 cup	60 mL

Combine first 3 ingredients in large bowl.

(continued on next page)

Side Dishes

Add potato. Toss until coated. Arrange in single layer on greased baking sheet with sides. Bake in 425°F (220°C) oven for about 30 minutes, turning once at halftime, until tender. Remove to same bowl.

Add pesto. Toss until coated. Serves 4.

1 serving: 281 Calories; 11.5 g Total Fat (2.5 g Mono, 0.4 g Poly, 1.8 g Sat); 4 mg Cholesterol; 38 g Carbohydrate; 4 g Fibre; 6 g Protein; 322 mg Sodium

Mediterranean Potatoes

Make merry on the Mediterranean with these well-seasoned, Italian-inspired spuds. Fantastico *with Lamb Meatball Skewers, page 118.*

Medium unpeeled potatoes, quartered	4	4
Grated Parmesan cheese	1/4 cup	60 mL
Sun-dried tomatoes in oil, blotted dry and chopped	3 tbsp.	50 mL
Olive (or cooking) oil	2 tbsp.	30 mL
Butter (or hard margarine), softened	2 tbsp.	30 mL
Garlic clove, minced (or 1/4 tsp., 1 mL, powder)	1	1
Dried crushed chilies	1/2 tsp.	2 mL
Salt	1/2 tsp.	2 mL
Dried rosemary, crushed	1/4 tsp.	1 mL
Dried whole oregano	1/4 tsp.	1 mL

Cook potato in boiling salted water in medium saucepan for about 10 minutes until partially cooked. Drain.

Combine remaining 9 ingredients in ungreased 2 quart (2 L) casserole. Add potato. Toss until coated. Cook, covered, in 375°F (190°C) oven for about 30 minutes until potato is tender. Serves 4.

1 serving: 218 Calories; 16.8 g Total Fat (8.5 g Mono, 1.2 g Poly, 6.0 g Sat); 20 mg Cholesterol; 12 g Carbohydrate; 5 g Fibre; 7 g Protein; 506 mg Sodium

Roasted Veggie Pockets

These pockets are a perfect fit for hands of all sizes. Partner with Herb-Scented Lamb Kabobs, page 121, for a fantastic Mediterranean-inspired meal.

Ranch dressing	1/4 cup	60 mL
Sliced green onion	2 tbsp.	30 mL
Lime juice	1 tbsp.	15 mL
Finely chopped chipotle pepper in adobo sauce (see Tip, below)	1 tsp.	5 mL
Asian eggplant, cut lengthwise into 1/4 inch (6 mm) slices	1	1
Medium zucchini, cut lengthwise into 1/4 inch (6 mm) slices	1	1
Medium red pepper, quartered	1	1
Olive (or cooking) oil	1 tbsp.	15 mL
Large tomato, cut in half	1	1
Olive (or cooking) oil	2 tsp.	10 mL
Whole wheat pita bread (7 inch, 18 cm, diameter), halved and opened	4	4

Combine first 4 ingredients in small bowl. Set aside.

Brush both sides of eggplant, zucchini and red pepper with first amount of olive oil. Arrange in single layer on greased baking sheet with sides.

Brush cut sides of tomato with second amount of olive oil. Place cut-side up on same baking sheet. Cook vegetables in 400°F (205°C) oven for 5 to 10 minutes until tender-crisp. Chop coarsely. Put into medium bowl. Add dressing mixture. Stir.

Place 1 pita half inside another to make a double-thick pocket. Repeat with remaining pita halves. Fill pockets with vegetable mixture. Serves 4.

1 serving: 336 Calories; 15.5 g Total Fat (4.4 g Mono, 1.3 g Poly, 2.3 g Sat); 4 mg Cholesterol; 46 g Carbohydrate; 8 g Fibre; 8 g Protein; 494 mg Sodium

 tip Chipotle chili peppers are smoked jalapeño peppers. Be sure to wash your hands after handling. To store any leftover chipotle chili peppers, divide into recipe-friendly portions and freeze, with sauce, in airtight containers for up to one year.

Maple-Glazed Vegetables

Put a truly Canadian spin on veggies by glazing them with maple syrup. Cut the potatoes about the same size as the carrots for even cooking. Cook alongside Lemon Herb Chicken, page 88.

Baby carrots	1 lb.	454 g
Baby potatoes, halved or quartered	1 lb.	454 g
Diced onion	1/2 cup	125 mL
Maple (or maple-flavoured) syrup	1/3 cup	75 mL
Finely grated gingerroot (or 1 1/2 tsp., 7 mL, ground ginger)	2 tbsp.	30 mL
Salt	1/2 tsp.	2 mL
Butter (or hard margarine)	2 tbsp.	30 mL
Lemon juice (optional)	2 tbsp.	30 mL
Chopped fresh parsley, for garnish		

Put first 6 ingredients into large bowl. Toss until vegetables are coated. Transfer to greased 2 quart (2 L) casserole.

Spoon dabs of butter, using 1/2 tsp. (2 mL) for each, over vegetable mixture. Bake, covered, in 375°F (190°C) oven for 30 to 40 minutes, stirring once at halftime, until vegetables are tender and glazed. Remove to large serving bowl.

Sprinkle with lemon juice. Toss.

Garnish with parsley. Serves 4.

1 serving: 253 Calories; 5.9 g Total Fat (1.5 g Mono, 0.3 g Poly, 3.6 g Sat); 15 mg Cholesterol; 46 g Carbohydrate; 5 g Fibre; 4 g Protein; 399 mg Sodium

CURRY-GLAZED VEGETABLES: Instead of gingerroot, use 1 to 2 tsp. (5 to 10 mL) curry powder. Sprinkle with orange juice instead of lemon juice.

HONEY-GARLIC GLAZED VEGETABLES: Use liquid honey instead of maple syrup, and dab with garlic butter instead of regular butter.

Braised Celery

*The often-unappreciated celery is dressed to impress with the
bold flavours of goat cheese and chili. This savoury side is
excellent with steamed rice and Artichoke Salmon, page 111.*

Cooking oil	1 tbsp.	15 mL
Celery ribs, cut into 1 inch (2.5 cm) pieces	8	8
Dried crushed chilies	1/4 tsp.	1 mL
Salt	1/4 tsp.	1 mL
Prepared chicken broth	3/4 cup	175 mL
Goat (chèvre) cheese	3 tbsp.	50 mL

Heat cooking oil in large frying pan on medium. Add next 3 ingredients.
Cook for about 5 minutes, stirring occasionally, until celery starts to soften.

Add broth. Stir. Bring to a boil. Boil gently, uncovered, for about 10 minutes
until celery is tender-crisp. Remove with slotted spoon to medium serving
bowl. Cover to keep warm. Boil remaining broth for 3 to 5 minutes until
reduced to about 1/4 cup (60 mL).

Add cheese. Heat and stir until smooth. Add to celery. Stir. Makes about
4 cups (1 L). Serves 6.

*1 serving: 51 Calories; 3.9 g Total Fat (1.8 g Mono, 0.8 g Poly, 1.2 g Sat); 4 mg Cholesterol;
2 g Carbohydrate; 1 g Fibre; 2 g Protein; 265 mg Sodium*

Variation: For even bolder flavour, use blue cheese instead of goat cheese.

Balsamic Onions

*Tangy and sweet, these onions make an elegant side for any grilled beef,
chicken or fish dish—add baked potatoes to make the meal complete.*

Large red onions, each cut into 8 wedges	2	2
Balsamic vinegar	1/4 cup	60 mL
Olive (or cooking) oil	2 tbsp.	30 mL
Brown sugar, packed	2 tbsp.	30 mL
Salt	1/2 tsp.	2 mL
Pepper	1/2 tsp.	2 mL

(continued on next page)

Arrange onion in single layer in ungreased 2 quart (2 L) shallow baking dish.

Combine next 3 ingredients in small cup. Drizzle over onion.

Sprinkle with salt and pepper. Bake, covered, in 400°F (205°C) oven for about 45 minutes until onion is softened. Bake, uncovered, for another 10 to 15 minutes until caramelized. Serves 4.

1 serving: 128 Calories; 6.8 g Total Fat (5.0 g Mono, 0.6 g Poly, 0.9 g Sat); 0 mg Cholesterol; 16 g Carbohydrate; 1 g Fibre; 1 g Protein; 303 mg Sodium

Garlicky Mashed Potatoes

Mashed potatoes need not be boring. They're easy to liven up with a little garlic and parsley. No gravy required here! Serve with Sweet Curry Sausages, page 64.

Peeled potatoes, cut up	3 lbs.	1.4 kg
Butter (or hard margarine)	1/3 cup	75 mL
Garlic cloves, minced (or 3/4 tsp., 4 mL, powder)	3	3
Milk	2/3 cup	150 mL
Pepper	1/4 tsp.	1 mL
Chopped fresh parsley (or 3/4 tsp., 4 mL, flakes)	1 tbsp.	15 mL

Cook potato in boiling salted water in large saucepan until tender. Drain.

Cover to keep warm.

Melt butter in small saucepan on medium. Add garlic. Cook for about 2 minutes, stirring constantly, until just golden. Add to potato.

Add milk and pepper. Mash. Remove to large serving bowl.

Sprinkle with parsley. Makes about 6 cups (1.5 L). Serves 4.

1 serving: 423 Calories; 15.2 g Total Fat (3.9 g Mono, 0.7 g Poly, 9.5 g Sat); 40 mg Cholesterol; 67 g Carbohydrate; 6 g Fibre; 7 g Protein; 139 mg Sodium

Sun-Dried Tomato Cornbread

Cornbread is given a modern makeover when it's speckled with sun-dried tomato and cheese. Ideal with Grilled Pork And Mango Salad, page 27.

All-purpose flour	1 1/2 cups	375 mL
Yellow cornmeal	1 cup	250 mL
Granulated sugar	1/4 cup	60 mL
Baking powder	2 tsp.	10 mL
Baking soda	1/2 tsp.	2 mL
Salt	1/2 tsp.	2 mL
Grated havarti cheese	1 cup	250 mL
Large eggs	2	2
Buttermilk (or soured milk, see Note)	1 cup	250 mL
Butter (or hard margarine), melted	1/2 cup	125 mL
Sun-dried tomatoes, softened in 1/2 cup boiling water for 10 minutes before finely chopping	1/2 cup	125 mL

Measure first 6 ingredients into large bowl. Stir.

Add cheese. Stir. Make a well in centre.

Combine remaining 4 ingredients in medium bowl. Add to well. Stir until just moistened. Spread in greased 8 x 8 inch (20 x 20 cm) pan. Bake in 350°F (175°C) oven for about 35 minutes until wooden pick inserted in centre comes out clean. Cuts into 9 pieces.

1 piece: 332 Calories; 16.5 g Total Fat (3.3 g Mono, 0.8 g Poly, 10.1 g Sat); 80 mg Cholesterol; 37 g Carbohydrate; 2 g Fibre; 8.5 g Protein; 503 mg Sodium

Pictured on page 53.

Note: To make soured milk, measure 1 tbsp. (15 mL) white vinegar or lemon juice into a 1 cup (250 mL) liquid measure. Add enough milk to make 1 cup (250 mL). Stir. Let stand for 1 minute.

Vegetable Spanish Rice

The refrain in Spain is that this dish is anything but plain! Top this tomato and pepper rice with a little salsa, and serve alongside Nacho-Crusted Haddock, page 109.

Cooking oil	2 tbsp.	30 mL
Finely chopped onion	1 cup	250 mL
Garlic cloves, minced (or 1/2 tsp., 2 mL, powder)	2	2
Long grain white rice	1 1/2 cups	375 mL
Prepared chicken (or vegetable) broth	2 1/2 cups	625 mL
Can of stewed tomatoes	14 oz.	398 mL
Diced green pepper	1 cup	250 mL
Paprika	1/2 tsp.	2 mL
Bay leaf	1	1

Heat cooking oil in large saucepan on medium. Add onion and garlic. Cook for 5 to 10 minutes, stirring often, until onion starts to soften.

Add rice. Stir until coated.

Add remaining 5 ingredients. Stir. Bring to a boil. Reduce heat to medium-low. Simmer, covered, for about 30 minutes, without stirring, until rice is tender and liquid is absorbed. Let stand for 5 minutes. Discard bay leaf. Fluff with a fork. Makes about 7 cups (1.75 L). Serves 6.

1 serving: 240 Calories; 5.2 g Total Fat (2.9 g Mono, 1.5 g Poly, 0.5 g Sat); 0 mg Cholesterol; 43 g Carbohydrate; 1 g Fibre; 6 g Protein; 475 mg Sodium

Paré Pointer

After a big heist, the thief hurried home and sawed the legs off his bed. He wanted to lie low for awhile.

Chipotle Cheese Potatoes

With 2 cheeses and smoky chipotle peppers, these potatoes have all the right stuffing! Great with Salmon With Avocado Salsa, page 110.

Large unpeeled baking potatoes	2	2
Chive and onion cream cheese	1/2 cup	125 mL
Grated medium Cheddar cheese	1/2 cup	125 mL
Finely chopped chipotle pepper in adobo sauce (see Tip, page 46)	1/2 tsp.	2 mL
Grated medium Cheddar cheese	1/4 cup	60 mL

Prick potatoes in several places with a fork. Wrap with paper towels. Microwave on high (100%) for about 10 minutes, turning once at halftime, until tender. Cut potatoes in half lengthwise. Scoop pulp into medium bowl, leaving 1/4 inch (6 mm) thick shells. Mash potato pulp.

Add next 3 ingredients. Stir. Spoon into shells. Place in ungreased 9 x 9 inch (22 x 22 cm) baking pan.

Sprinkle with second amount of Cheddar cheese. Bake in 375°F (190°C) oven for 20 to 30 minutes until heated through. Serves 4.

1 serving: 335 Calories; 17.3 g Total Fat (2.0 g Mono, 0.3 g Poly, 11.5 g Sat); 52 mg Cholesterol; 34 g Carbohydrate; 3 g Fibre; 10 g Protein; 282 mg Sodium

GRILLED CHIPOTLE CHEESE POTATOES: Preheat gas barbecue to medium. Place sheet of heavy-duty (or double layer of regular) foil on ungreased grill. Place stuffed potatoes on foil. Close lid. Cook for about 25 minutes until heated through and cheese is golden.

Pictured on page 108.

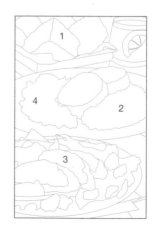

Spiced Yam Hash

Regular hash browns a bit too blasé? Switch the potatoes for
yams and perk the whole thing up with a sweet, spicy heat.
Tastes great with Ribbon Zucchini Frittata, page 140.

Cooking oil	2 tbsp.	30 mL
Cubed peeled yam (or sweet potato)	3 cups	750 mL
Chopped green onion	1/2 cup	125 mL
Chopped red pepper	1/2 cup	125 mL
Paprika	1/2 tsp.	2 mL
Chili powder	1/2 tsp.	2 mL
Salt	1/2 tsp.	2 mL
Ground cinnamon	1/8 tsp.	0.5 mL

Heat cooking oil in medium frying pan on medium-high. Add yam.
Heat and stir for about 5 minutes until starting to brown. Reduce heat
to medium-low.

Add remaining 6 ingredients. Stir. Cook, covered, for about 5 minutes,
stirring occasionally, until yam is tender. Makes about 2 1/2 cups (625 mL).
Serves 4.

1 serving: 202 Calories; 7.2 g Total Fat (4.0 g Mono, 2.2 g Poly, 0.6 g Sat); 0 mg Cholesterol;
33 g Carbohydrate; 5 g Fibre; 2 g Protein; 308 mg Sodium

Pictured at left.

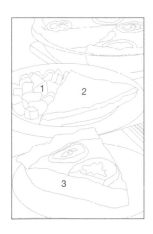

1. Spiced Yam Hash, above
2. Ribbon Zucchini Frittata, page 140
3. Curried Tuna Quiche, page 98

Props courtesy of: The Bay

Potato Vegetable Kabobs

There's always time to enhance the natural flavours of grilled veggies with lime.
Make it a citrus-themed night and serve with Margarita Marinated Steak, page 74.

Lime juice	1/4 cup	60 mL
Orange juice	2 tbsp.	30 mL
Sun-dried tomato pesto	2 tbsp.	30 mL
Cooking oil	2 tbsp.	30 mL
White baby potatoes, larger ones cut in half	1 1/2 lbs.	680 g
Large red peppers, cut into 1 1/2 inch (3.8 cm) pieces	2	2
Medium zucchini (with peel), halved lengthwise and cut into 1 inch (2.5 cm) slices	2	2
Bamboo skewers (8 inches, 20 cm, each), soaked in water for 10 minutes	12	12

Combine first 4 ingredients in small cup. Set aside.

Put potatoes on microwave-safe plate. Microwave on high (100%) for about 5 minutes until just tender.

Thread potatoes, red pepper and zucchini alternately onto skewers. Place on large plate. Brush kabobs with half of lime juice mixture. Preheat gas barbecue to medium (see Tip, below). Cook kabobs on greased grill for about 15 minutes, turning once at halftime and brushing with remaining lime juice mixture, until vegetables are tender-crisp. Serves 6.

1 serving: 117 Calories; 5.9 g Total Fat (3.4 g Mono, 1.6 g Poly, 0.5 g Sat); 0 mg Cholesterol; 14 g Carbohydrate; 5 g Fibre; 4 g Protein; 36 mg Sodium

Pictured on page 72.

 tip   Too cold to barbecue? Use the broiler instead! Your food should cook in about the same length of time—and remember to turn or baste as directed. Set your oven rack so that the food is about 3 to 4 inches (7.5 to 10 cm) away from the top element—for most ovens, this is the top rack.

Smashed Celery Spuds

*These unique celery, cauliflower and onion potatoes are simply
smashing! Serve with Cheese And Pesto Meatloaf, page 70.*

Peeled potatoes, cut up	1 1/2 lbs.	680 g
Butter (or hard margarine)	2 tbsp.	30 mL
Chopped cauliflower	2 cups	500 mL
Finely chopped celery	1 cup	250 mL
Finely chopped onion	1/2 cup	125 mL
Prepared chicken broth	1/3 cup	75 mL
Milk	1/4 cup	60 mL
Butter (or hard margarine)	2 tbsp.	30 mL
Pepper	1/4 tsp.	1 mL

Cook potato in boiling salted water in large saucepan until tender. Drain.
Return to same saucepan. Heat on medium-low, shaking saucepan, until
potato is dry. Remove from heat. Cover to keep warm.

Melt first amount of butter in medium saucepan on medium. Add next
3 ingredients. Cook, covered, for 5 to 10 minutes, stirring occasionally,
until vegetables are tender-crisp.

Add broth. Stir. Cook, covered, for 3 to 5 minutes until vegetables are
tender. Add to potato.

Add remaining 3 ingredients. Mash. Makes about 4 3/4 cups (1.2 L).
Serves 4.

*1 serving: 282 Calories; 11.9 g Total Fat (3.1 g Mono, 0.6 g Poly, 7.4 g Sat); 31 mg Cholesterol;
41 g Carbohydrate; 5 g Fibre; 5 g Protein; 490 mg Sodium*

Pictured on page 71.

Paré Pointer
*When she heard there was going to be some change in
the weather, she walked around with an open purse.*

Sweet And Spicy Onions

*Caramelized onions make a simply sweet (and spicy) side
for Tangy Chicken Potato Bake page 91.*

Butter (or hard margarine), softened	3 tbsp.	50 mL
Chili sauce	2 tbsp.	30 mL
Brown sugar, packed	1 tbsp.	15 mL
Worcestershire sauce	1 tsp.	5 mL
Salt	1/8 tsp.	0.5 mL
Pepper	1/8 tsp.	0.5 mL
Medium onions, each cut into 4 wedges	4	4
Grated Parmesan cheese	2 tsp.	10 mL

Melt butter in large frying pan on medium. Add next 5 ingredients. Heat
and stir until bubbling.

Add onion. Stir to coat. Cook, covered, for about 30 minutes, stirring
occasionally, until onion is very soft and caramelized.

Sprinkle with cheese. Makes about 3 cups (750 mL). Serves 4.

*1 serving: 142 Calories; 9.0 g Total Fat (2.3 g Mono, 0.4 g Poly, 5.6 g Sat); 23 mg Cholesterol;
15 g Carbohydrate; 2 g Fibre; 2 g Protein; 161 mg Sodium*

Goat Cheese Crostini

*Looking for something light for dinner? Serve with Seafood Spinach Salad, page 37,
and you're all set. Need an appealing appetizer? Slice the baguette on the diagonal
for a stylish presentation and double the recipe to use the entire loaf.*

Baguette bread slices (about 1/2 inch, 12 mm, thick)	12	12
Olive (or cooking) oil	2 tbsp.	30 mL
Balsamic vinegar	1 tsp.	5 mL
Goat (chèvre) cheese, room temperature	1/2 cup	125 mL
Coarsely ground pepper	1/4 tsp.	1 mL

Arrange bread slices on ungreased baking sheet with sides.

(continued on next page)

Side Dishes

Combine olive oil and vinegar in small cup. Brush on bread. Bake in 350°F (175°C) oven for about 10 minutes until toasted.

Spread cheese on toast. Broil on top rack in oven for about 2 minutes until cheese is melted.

Sprinkle with pepper. Serves 4 to 6.

1 serving: 336 Calories; 10.7 g Total Fat (5.9 g Mono, 0.7 g Poly, 3.6 g Sat); 9 mg Cholesterol; 47 g Carbohydrate; 1 g Fibre; 11 g Protein; 624 mg Sodium

SUN-DRIED TOMATO CROSTINI: Combine goat cheese with 1 tbsp. (15 mL) sun-dried tomato pesto before spreading on toast.

Pictured on page 36 and on back cover.

Lemon Pepper Greens

This crisp and colourful side will leave other dishes green with envy.
Simply sinful with Scallop "Orzotto," page 103.

Butter (or hard margarine)	1 tbsp.	15 mL
Cooking oil	1 tsp.	5 mL
Sugar snap peas, trimmed	2 cups	500 mL
Chopped fresh (or frozen) green beans	2 cups	500 mL
Fresh asparagus, trimmed of tough ends and cut into 1 inch (2.5 cm) pieces	1 lb.	454 g
Lemon juice	1 tbsp.	15 mL
Lemon pepper	1 tsp.	5 mL
Pine nuts, toasted (see Tip, page 20), optional	2 tbsp.	30 mL

Heat wok or large frying pan on medium-high until very hot. Add butter and cooking oil. Add next 3 ingredients. Stir-fry for 3 to 4 minutes until vegetables are tender-crisp.

Add remaining 3 ingredients. Stir. Makes about 5 cups (1.25 L). Serves 4.

1 serving: 112 Calories; 4.3 g Total Fat (1.4 g Mono, 0.6 g Poly, 1.9 g Sat); 8 mg Cholesterol; 15 g Carbohydrate; 5 g Fibre; 5 g Protein; 64 mg Sodium

Lemon-Kissed Couscous

They'll be lining up to kiss the cook when you serve them this colourful couscous.
Delightful when served warm or cold with Satay Pork Skewers, page 141.

Cooking oil	1 tsp.	5 mL
Chopped fennel bulb (white part only)	1 1/4 cups	300 mL
Garlic clove, minced (or 1/4 tsp., 1 mL, powder)	1	1
Prepared chicken broth	1 1/2 cups	375 mL
Frozen peas	1 cup	250 mL
Plain couscous	1 cup	250 mL
Diced tomato	3/4 cup	175 mL
Dark raisins	1/2 cup	125 mL
Lemon juice	2 tbsp.	30 mL
Grated lemon zest	1/2 tsp.	2 mL

Heat cooking oil in large frying pan on medium. Add fennel and garlic. Cook for about 5 minutes, stirring often, until fennel is tender-crisp.

Add broth and peas. Stir. Bring to a boil.

Add remaining 5 ingredients. Stir. Remove from heat. Let stand, covered, for about 5 minutes until couscous is tender and broth is absorbed. Fluff with a fork. Makes about 5 cups (1.25 L). Serves 4.

1 serving: 332 Calories; 2.5 g Total Fat (1.0 g Mono, 0.7 g Poly, 0.4 g Sat); 0 mg Cholesterol; 68 g Carbohydrate; 8 g Fibre; 12 g Protein; 401 mg Sodium

Paré Pointer
Cross a termite and a praying mantis and you get
a bug that says grace before eating your house.

Baked Fragrant Rice

With a name like this, you know your kitchen is going to smell wonderful once you get cooking. Pair with Pork In Plum Sauce, page 137.

Cooking oil	2 tbsp.	30 mL
Chopped onion	1 cup	250 mL
Long grain white rice	1 1/2 cups	375 mL
Garlic clove, minced (or 1/4 tsp., 1 mL, powder)	1	1
Finely grated gingerroot (or 1/8 tsp., 0.5 mL, ground ginger)	1/2 tsp.	2 mL
Garam masala (see Tip, below)	1/2 tsp.	2 mL
Chopped butternut squash	2 1/2 cups	625 mL
Prepared chicken broth	2 1/2 cups	625 mL
Chopped pistachios	1/4 cup	60 mL

Heat cooking oil in large frying pan on medium. Add onion. Cook for 5 to 10 minutes, stirring often, until softened.

Add next 4 ingredients. Heat and stir for about 3 minutes until fragrant. Transfer to ungreased 2 quart (2 L) casserole.

Add remaining 3 ingredients. Stir. Bake, covered, in 375°F (190°C) oven for about 1 hour until squash and rice are tender and broth is absorbed. Fluff with a fork. Makes about 8 cups (2 L). Serves 6.

1 serving: 295 Calories; 7.6 g Total Fat (4.1 g Mono, 2.2 g Poly, 0.8 g Sat); 0 mg Cholesterol; 52 g Carbohydrate; 3 g Fibre; 7 g Protein; 328 mg Sodium

 tip If you don't keep garam masala on hand, add just a pinch each of ground cumin, coriander, pepper, cardamom, cinnamon and cloves.

Cabbage Noodles

An unexpected combination of coleslaw and noodles makes a super simple side for supper. Excellent with Herb-Scented Lamb Kabobs, page 121.

Broad egg noodles	3 cups	750 mL
Olive (or cooking) oil	1 tbsp.	15 mL
Butter (or hard margarine)	1 tbsp.	15 mL
Coleslaw mix (about 1 lb., 454 g)	8 cups	2 L
Thinly sliced onion	1 cup	250 mL
Granulated sugar	1 tbsp.	15 mL
Garlic clove, minced (or 1/4 tsp., 1 mL, powder)	1	1
Salt	1/2 tsp.	2 mL
Pepper	1/4 tsp.	1 mL

Cook noodles in boiling salted water in large uncovered saucepan for 6 to 8 minutes, stirring occasionally, until tender but firm. Drain. Return to same pot. Cover to keep warm.

Heat olive oil and butter in Dutch oven on medium. Add remaining 6 ingredients. Cook, covered, for about 10 minutes, stirring occasionally, until coleslaw is softened. Add noodles. Stir. Makes about 6 cups (1.5 L). Serves 4.

1 serving: 223 Calories; 7.5 g Total Fat (3.6 g Mono, 0.8 g Poly, 2.6 g Sat); 31 mg Cholesterol; 33 g Carbohydrate; 4 g Fibre; 6 g Protein; 353 mg Sodium

Pictured on page 17.

Sweet Sugar Peas

Indulge your sweet tooth with this quick and easy side of tender-crisp pea pods coated in a sweet, gingery glaze. Delicious with Peanut Chicken Rice Bake, page 87.

Frozen concentrated orange juice, thawed	2 tbsp.	30 mL
Water	1 tbsp.	15 mL
Soy sauce	2 tsp.	10 mL
Cornstarch	1 tsp.	5 mL
Ground ginger	1/4 tsp.	1 mL
Cooking oil	2 tsp.	10 mL
Sugar snap peas, trimmed	5 cups	1.25 L

(continued on next page)

Combine first 5 ingredients in small cup.

Heat cooking oil in large frying pan on medium. Add peas. Heat and stir for about 5 minutes until tender-crisp. Stir cornstarch mixture. Add to peas. Heat and stir for about 1 minute until sauce is thickened. Makes about 4 cups (1 L). Serves 6.

1 serving: 80 Calories; 1.5 g Total Fat (0.9 g Mono, 0.5 g Poly, 0.1 g Sat); 0 mg Cholesterol; 12 g Carbohydrate; 3 g Fibre; 3 g Protein; 160 mg Sodium

Creamed Spinach

Put a whole new spin on spinach with the addition of prosciutto and nutmeg. Serve with Moroccan Pot Roast, page 66, and steamed carrots.

Cooking oil	2 tbsp.	30 mL
Chopped prosciutto (or deli) ham	1/2 cup	125 mL
Butter (or hard margarine)	1/4 cup	60 mL
Finely chopped onion	1 1/3 cups	325 mL
Garlic cloves, minced (or 1 tsp., 5 mL, powder)	4	4
Coarsely chopped fresh spinach, lightly packed	12 cups	3 L
Sour cream	1 cup	250 mL
Ground nutmeg	1/2 tsp.	2 mL

Heat cooking oil in Dutch oven on medium. Add ham. Heat and stir for 3 to 5 minutes until crisp. Transfer to small bowl. Set aside. Reduce heat to medium-low.

Melt butter in same pan. Add onion and garlic. Cook for about 5 minutes, stirring often, until onion is softened.

Add spinach. Heat and stir for 1 to 2 minutes until spinach is almost wilted.

Add ham, sour cream and nutmeg. Heat and stir for 1 minute. Makes about 4 cups (1 L). Serves 8.

1 serving: 195 Calories; 15.9 g Total Fat (3.5 g Mono, 1.3 g Poly, 7.9 g Sat); 46 mg Cholesterol; 6 g Carbohydrate; 1 g Fibre; 7 g Protein; 467 mg Sodium

Sweet Curry Sausages

*Just call them Bangalore Bangers! Ordinary sausages go
down India way with apple, raisins and a coconut curry flavour.
Great with Garlicky Mashed Potatoes, page 49.*

Prepared chicken broth	1/4 cup	60 mL
Cornstarch	1 tsp.	5 mL
Cooking oil	2 tsp.	10 mL
Beef sausages, casings removed, cut into 1 inch (2.5 cm) pieces	1 lb.	454 g
Chopped peeled tart apple (such as Granny Smith)	2 cups	500 mL
Sliced onion	1 cup	250 mL
Garlic cloves, minced (or 1/2 tsp., 2 mL, powder)	2	2
Finely grated gingerroot (or 1/4 tsp., 1 mL, ground ginger)	1 tsp.	5 mL
Curry powder	1 1/2 tbsp.	25 mL
Can of light coconut milk	14 oz.	398 mL
Dark raisins	1/3 cup	75 mL

Stir broth into cornstarch in small cup. Set aside.

Heat cooking oil in large frying pan on medium-high. Add sausage. Cook
for about 5 minutes, stirring occasionally, until browned. Drain. Reduce
heat to medium.

Add next 4 ingredients. Cook for about 5 minutes, stirring occasionally,
until apple starts to soften.

Add curry powder. Heat and stir for about 1 minute until fragrant.

Add coconut milk and raisins. Stir. Bring to a boil. Reduce heat to medium.
Boil gently, uncovered, for about 5 minutes, stirring occasionally, until apple
is tender. Stir cornstarch mixture. Add to sausage mixture. Heat and stir
for about 1 minute until boiling and thickened. Makes about 4 cups (1 L).
Serves 4.

*1 serving: 553 Calories; 40.9 g Total Fat (15.8 g Mono, 1.7 g Poly, 18.1 g Sat); 93 mg Cholesterol;
25 g Carbohydrate; 2 g Fibre; 22 g Protein; 792 mg Sodium*

Family Fajitas

Every aspiring señor and señorita loves a steak-filled fajita.
Serve with all the fixings that make do-it-yourself fajitas
so fun—lettuce, grated cheese, sour cream and salsa.

Paprika	1 tsp.	5 mL
Seasoned salt	1/2 tsp.	2 mL
Garlic powder	1/2 tsp.	2 mL
Ground cumin	1/2 tsp.	2 mL
Dry mustard	1/4 tsp.	1 mL
Cayenne pepper, just a pinch		
Flour tortillas (7 1/2 inch, 19 cm, diameter)	8	8
Cooking oil	1 tbsp.	15 mL
Beef top sirloin steak, cut into short strips	1 lb.	454 g
Cooking oil	1 tsp.	5 mL
Sliced fresh white mushrooms	2 cups	500 mL
Thinly sliced onion	1 cup	250 mL
Thinly sliced red pepper	1 cup	250 mL
Thinly sliced yellow pepper	1 cup	250 mL

Combine first 6 ingredients in small cup. Set aside.

Wrap tortillas in foil. Heat in 425°F (220°C) oven for 10 to 15 minutes until warm.

Heat first amount of cooking oil in large frying pan on medium. Add beef. Sprinkle with 2 tsp. (10 mL) spice mixture. Stir. Cook for about 5 minutes, stirring occasionally, until beef is browned. Transfer to large bowl. Set aside.

Heat second amount of cooking oil in same frying pan. Add mushrooms and onion. Cook for 5 to 10 minutes, stirring often, until onion is softened.

Add red and yellow peppers. Stir. Sprinkle with remaining spice mixture. Cook for about 5 minutes, stirring occasionally, until peppers are tender-crisp. Add beef. Heat and stir until heated through. Arrange beef mixture down centre of tortillas. Fold bottom ends of tortillas over filling. Fold in sides, slightly overlapping, leaving top ends open. Serves 4.

1 serving: 618 Calories; 23.6 g Total Fat (11.0 g Mono, 3.5 g Poly, 6.5 g Sat); 83 mg Cholesterol; 57 g Carbohydrate; 5 g Fibre; 43 g Protein; 871 mg Sodium

Moroccan Pot Roast

Spice up your Sunday night roast with exotic flavours—your taste buds will be rockin' to the Moroccan experience. Steam some carrots and serve with Creamed Spinach, page 63.

Olive (or cooking) oil	2 tbsp.	30 mL
Ground cumin	1 tsp.	5 mL
Ground coriander	1 tsp.	5 mL
Ground ginger	1 tsp.	5 mL
Granulated sugar	1 tsp.	5 mL
Salt	1 tsp.	5 mL
Garlic powder	1/2 tsp.	2 mL
Ground cinnamon	1/2 tsp.	2 mL
Boneless beef cross-rib roast	3 lbs.	1.4 kg
Red baby potatoes, larger ones cut in half	2 lbs.	900 g
Prepared beef broth	1 cup	250 mL
Water	1/3 cup	75 mL
All-purpose flour	2 tbsp.	30 mL

Combine first 8 ingredients in small bowl.

Rub spice mixture on roast. Place on greased wire rack set in large roasting pan. Bake, uncovered, in 450°F (230°C) oven for about 30 minutes, turning once at halftime, until browned. Reduce heat to 350°F (175°C).

Arrange potatoes around roast in pan. Bake, covered, for another 1 to 1 1/2 hours until potatoes are tender and meat thermometer inserted into thickest part of roast reads 160°F (71°C) for medium or until desired doneness. Remove roast to cutting board. Cover with foil. Let stand for 10 minutes. Stir potatoes gently in pan until coated with drippings. Remove with slotted spoon to large serving bowl. Cover to keep warm.

Transfer remaining drippings to medium saucepan. Add broth. Stir. Bring to a boil.

Stir water into flour in small cup until smooth. Slowly add to broth mixture, stirring constantly until boiling and thickened. Strain through sieve into small serving bowl. Cut roast into thin slices. Makes 12 servings (2 to 3 oz., 57 to 85 g each, cooked weight). Serve with potatoes and gravy. Serves 12.

1 serving: 383 Calories; 27.0 g Total Fat (12.1 g Mono, 1.2 g Poly, 10.3 g Sat); 70 mg Cholesterol; 14 g Carbohydrate; 1 g Fibre; 20 g Protein; 320 mg Sodium

Bruschetta Steak Loaf

Plain old steak sandwiches are given a makeover with fresh tomatoes and peppers. Sure to please when served with Orange Basil Broccoli, page 44. Use the remaining bread another day to make garlic toast.

French bread loaf	1/2	1/2
Sun-dried tomato pesto	1/4 cup	60 mL
Chopped tomato	1 1/2 cups	375 mL
Finely diced green pepper	1/2 cup	125 mL
Finely chopped green onion	2 tbsp.	30 mL
Italian dressing	1 tbsp.	15 mL
Italian dressing	1/4 cup	60 mL
Beef strip loin steak, cut crosswise into short strips	1 lb.	454 g
Pepper	1/2 tsp.	2 mL
Chopped fresh basil	2 tbsp.	30 mL

Cut bread in half lengthwise. Cut crosswise to make 4 pieces. Place cut-side up on ungreased baking sheet. Broil on centre rack in oven for about 1 minute until golden. Spread pesto on cut sides of bread.

Combine next 4 ingredients in medium bowl. Spoon tomato mixture over pesto.

Heat 2 tbsp. (30 mL) dressing in large frying pan on medium-high. Add beef. Sprinkle with pepper. Stir-fry for 3 to 4 minutes until desired doneness. Remove from heat. Stir in remaining dressing. Spoon beef over tomato mixture.

Sprinkle with basil. Serves 4.

1 serving: 743 Calories; 36.5 g Total Fat (17.7 g Mono, 6.2 g Poly, 9.0 g Sat); 75 mg Cholesterol; 68 g Carbohydrate; 6 g Fibre; 35 g Protein; 1097 mg Sodium

Tortellini Chili Bake

A can of chili, a package of fresh tortellini and some chopped-up veggies are all you need for a hearty meal on busy evenings. Sprinkle with sliced green onion or grated Cheddar cheese for a colourful, tasty garnish.

Chopped tomato	2 cups	500 mL
Tomato juice	2 cups	500 mL
Can of chili (see Note)	15 oz.	425 g
Chopped green pepper	1 1/3 cups	325 mL
Finely chopped onion	1/4 cup	60 mL
Cream cheese, cut up	1/4 cup	60 mL
Package of fresh beef-filled tortellini	12 1/2 oz.	350 g

Combine first 6 ingredients in greased 2 quart (2 L) casserole.

Add tortellini. Stir gently. Bake, covered, in 425°F (220°C) oven for about 45 minutes, stirring once at halftime, until tortellini is tender but firm. Makes about 8 cups (2 L). Serves 4.

1 serving: 392 Calories; 15.3 g Total Fat (4.0 g Mono, 0.7 g Poly, 8.2 g Sat); 61 mg Cholesterol; 51 g Carbohydrate; 8 g Fibre; 17 g Protein; 1380 mg Sodium

Pictured on page 89.

Note: Instead of canned chili, use 2 cups (500 mL) leftover chili.

Paré Pointer

If oxygen was only discovered in the seventeen hundreds, what did people breathe before then?

Entrees – Beef

Beef And Bowtie Pasta

Bowtie pasta is all dressed up with tangy balsamic vinaigrette and sharp Dijon.
Serve this meaty pasta with a side of veggies or over fresh spinach leaves for
a complete meal. Can be chilled or served at room temperature.

Medium bow pasta	2 1/2 cups	625 mL
Diced red pepper	1/4 cup	60 mL
Chopped fresh parsley	1/4 cup	60 mL
Cooking oil	1 tbsp.	15 mL
Beef top sirloin steak, cut diagonally into 1/4 inch (6 mm) slices	1 lb.	454 g
Balsamic vinaigrette	1/2 cup	125 mL
Dijon mustard (with whole seeds)	2 tbsp.	30 mL
Capers (optional)	2 tbsp.	30 mL

Cook pasta in boiling salted water in large uncovered saucepan or Dutch oven for 8 to 10 minutes, stirring occasionally, until tender but firm. Drain. Rinse with cold water. Drain well. Transfer to large bowl.

Add red pepper and parsley. Toss. Set aside.

Heat cooking oil in large frying pan on medium-high. Add beef. Cook for 3 minutes, stirring constantly.

Add remaining 3 ingredients. Cook for 1 to 2 minutes, scraping any brown bits from bottom of pan, until desired doneness. Add to pasta mixture. Toss. Makes about 6 cups (1.5 L). Serves 4.

1 serving: 506 Calories; 26.5 g Total Fat (8.2 g Mono, 1.6 g Poly, 7.2 g Sat); 53 mg Cholesterol; 36 g Carbohydrate; 1 g Fibre; 29 g Protein; 461 mg Sodium

Cheese And Pesto Meatloaf

Is your family pesto-ing you for dinner? Pesto them back with this hearty meatloaf. Perfect served with Smashed Celery Spuds, page 57. And you'll have just enough meatloaf left over for sandwiches the next day!

Large eggs, fork-beaten	2	2
Finely chopped onion	3/4 cup	175 mL
Fine dry bread crumbs	2/3 cup	150 mL
Finely chopped green pepper	1/2 cup	125 mL
Grated carrot	1/2 cup	125 mL
Sun-dried tomato pesto	3 tbsp.	50 mL
Salt	1 tsp.	5 mL
Pepper	1/2 tsp.	2 mL
Lean ground beef	1 1/2 lbs.	680 g
Sun-dried tomato pesto	2 tbsp.	30 mL
Grated medium Cheddar cheese	1/2 cup	125 mL

Combine first 8 ingredients in large bowl.

Add beef. Mix well. Press into ungreased 9 × 5 × 3 inch (22 × 12.5 × 7.5 cm) loaf pan. Bake in 350°F (175°C) oven for about 1 hour until fully cooked, and internal temperature of beef reaches 160°F (71°C).

Spread second amount of pesto on meatloaf. Sprinkle with cheese. Bake for another 5 to 10 minutes until cheese is melted. Let stand for 10 minutes. Serves 6.

1 serving: 398 Calories; 23.7 g Total Fat (10.5 g Mono, 1.3 g Poly, 9.2 g Sat); 140 mg Cholesterol; 17 g Carbohydrate; 2 g Fibre; 29 g Protein; 698 mg Sodium

Pictured at right.

1. Cheese and Pesto Meatloaf, above
2. Smashed Celery Spuds, page 57
3. Pork Pot Roast, page 138

Props courtesy of: Cherison Enterprises Inc.
Danesco Inc.
Pfaltzgraff Canada

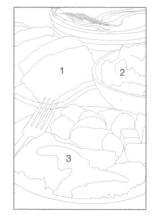

Meatball Shepherd's Pie

Shepherd's pie is extra-fun for the family when meatballs are involved. Customize this dish by using your favourite pasta sauce and cheese, or try meatballs made with ground chicken or turkey.

Frozen cooked meatballs	32	32
Roasted garlic tomato pasta sauce	2 cups	500 mL
Chopped zucchini (with peel)	2 cups	500 mL
Chopped green pepper	1 cup	250 mL
Frozen hash brown potatoes	3 cups	750 mL
Crumbled feta cheese	1 cup	250 mL
Sour cream	1/2 cup	125 mL
Grated Parmesan cheese	1/4 cup	60 mL
Dried oregano	1/2 tsp.	2 mL

Combine first 4 ingredients in ungreased 2 quart (2 L) casserole.

Combine remaining 5 ingredients in large bowl. Spoon onto meatball mixture. Bake, covered, in 375°F (190°C) oven for 1 hour. Bake, uncovered, for another 20 to 30 minutes until heated through. Serves 4.

1 serving: 630 Calories; 31.8 g Total Fat (8.7 g Mono, 1.5 g Poly, 16.0 g Sat); 154 mg Cholesterol; 52 g Carbohydrate; 6 g Fibre; 34 g Protein; 1021 mg Sodium

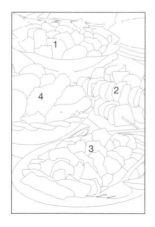

1. Herbed Potato Salad, page 13
2. Potato Vegetable Kabobs, page 56
3. Margarita Marinated Steak, page 74
4. Crispy Chicken Drumettes, page 84

Props courtesy of: Stokes

Margarita Marinated Steak

Give a less-tender cut of meat the spa treatment with a long soak in a refreshing lime-scented marinade, and watch it become tender and juicy. Complete this makeover with a pitcher of margaritas and Potato Vegetable Kabobs, page 56, on the side.

Frozen concentrated limeade, thawed	1/3 cup	75 mL
Water	1/3 cup	75 mL
Cooking oil	1/4 cup	60 mL
Chopped fresh cilantro	1/4 cup	60 mL
Cajun seasoning	3 tbsp.	50 mL
Garlic cloves, minced (or 3/4 tsp., 4 mL, powder)	3	3
Ground cumin	1 tsp.	5 mL
Boneless beef round steak, trimmed of fat	1 1/2 lbs.	680 g
Chopped avocado	1 cup	250 mL
Chopped orange	3/4 cup	175 mL
Finely chopped red onion	1/4 cup	60 mL

Combine first 7 ingredients in small bowl. Reserve 2 tbsp. (30 mL) in small cup.

Put beef into large resealable freezer bag. Add remaining limeade mixture. Seal bag. Turn until coated. Let stand in refrigerator for at least 6 hours or overnight, turning occasionally. Drain. Preheat gas barbecue to medium (see Tip, page 56). Cook beef on greased grill for about 3 minutes per side for medium-rare or until desired doneness. Remove to cutting board. Cover to keep warm.

Combine remaining 3 ingredients in small bowl. Add reserved limeade mixture. Toss until coated. Cut beef diagonally into 1/4 inch (6 mm) slices. Arrange on large serving plate. Top with avocado mixture. Serves 6.

1 serving: 268 Calories; 13.7 g Total Fat (7.1 g Mono, 1.4 g Poly, 3.8 g Sat); 55 mg Cholesterol; 8 g Carbohydrate; 2 g Fibre; 28 g Protein; 269 mg Sodium

Pictured on page 72.

Beef And Mushroom Arugula

Arugula, popular for its peppery mustard flavour,
is a must try for the stir-fry fan. Pair with pasta.

Cooking oil	1 tsp.	5 mL
Beef rib-eye steak, cut into 1 inch (2.5 cm) pieces	1 lb.	454 g
Butter (or hard margarine)	2 tbsp.	30 mL
Chopped onion	1/3 cup	75 mL
Garlic clove, minced (or 1/4 tsp., 1 mL, powder)	1	1
Sliced brown (or white) mushrooms	2 cups	500 mL
Fresh arugula, stems removed, coarsely chopped, lightly packed	4 cups	1 L
Sour cream	1/4 cup	60 mL
Salt	1/4 tsp.	1 mL
Pepper	1/8 tsp.	0.5 mL

Heat cooking oil in large frying pan on medium-high. Add beef. Cook for about 3 minutes, stirring occasionally, until desired doneness. Transfer to large bowl. Set aside.

Melt butter in same frying pan on medium. Add onion and garlic. Cook for about 5 minutes, stirring often, until onion is softened.

Add mushrooms. Stir. Cook for 5 to 10 minutes, stirring occasionally, until mushrooms are softened.

Add beef and remaining 4 ingredients. Heat and stir for about 1 minute until heated through and arugula is wilted. Makes about 4 cups (1 L). Serves 4.

1 serving: 373 Calories; 28.0 g Total Fat (10.1 g Mono, 1.3 g Poly, 13.0 g Sat); 85 mg Cholesterol; 4 g Carbohydrate; 1 g Fibre; 25 g Protein; 259 mg Sodium

Hamburger Pizza

This hamburger-pizza combo upgrades all notions of the takeout favourite.
Sure to thrill kids of all ages. Easily doubled, if you're so inclined.

Cooking oil	1 tsp.	5 mL
Sliced fresh white mushrooms	1 cup	250 mL
Chopped onion	1/2 cup	125 mL
Lean ground beef	1/4 lb.	113 g
Dried basil	1/4 tsp.	1 mL
Prebaked pizza crust (12 inch, 30 cm, diameter)	1	1
Pizza (or pasta) sauce	1/4 cup	60 mL
Grated Parmesan cheese	1/4 cup	60 mL
Medium tomato, seeds removed, chopped	1	1
Grated mozzarella cheese	1 cup	250 mL

Heat cooking oil in medium frying pan on medium. Add next 4 ingredients. Scramble-fry for about 10 minutes until beef is no longer pink. Remove from heat. Drain.

Place pizza crust on 12 inch (30 cm) pizza pan. Spread pizza sauce on crust almost to edge.

Sprinkle with Parmesan cheese.

Scatter beef mixture, tomato and mozzarella cheese over top. Bake in 450°F (230°C) oven for 10 to 15 minutes until crust is crisp and cheese is melted. Serves 4.

1 serving: 436 Calories; 15.4 g Total Fat (4.0 g Mono, 0.8 g Poly, 6.5 g Sat); 43 mg Cholesterol; 50 g Carbohydrate; 3 g Fibre; 24 g Protein; 791 mg Sodium

Italian Steak Dinner

They'll think they've been to Tuscany after they've dined on this delectable dinner! Fabulous with Marinated Mushroom Salad, page 8.

Jar of marinated artichoke hearts, drained, liquid reserved, finely chopped	6 oz.	170 mL
Sun-dried tomatoes, softened in boiling water for 10 minutes before finely chopping	1/4 cup	60 mL
Reserved artichoke liquid	1/3 cup	75 mL
Pepper	1 tsp.	5 mL
Fennel seed	1/2 tsp.	2 mL
Dried oregano	1/2 tsp.	2 mL
Beef strip loin steak, cut into 4 equal pieces	1 lb.	454 g
Polenta roll, cut into 8 slices	1.1 lbs.	500 g
Olive (or cooking) oil	1 tbsp.	15 mL

Put artichoke hearts and sun-dried tomato into small bowl. Add half of artichoke marinade. Stir. Set aside.

Add next 3 ingredients to remaining artichoke marinade. Stir.

Brush both sides of beef with fennel mixture.

Brush both sides of polenta with olive oil. Place steak and polenta on greased broiler pan. Broil on top rack in oven for 3 to 5 minutes per side for medium-rare or until desired doneness. Transfer to large serving plate. Top polenta with artichoke mixture. Serves 4.

1 serving: 420 Calories; 23.9 g Total Fat (9.8 g Mono, 1.0 g Poly, 7.4 g Sat); 62 mg Cholesterol; 26 g Carbohydrate; 2 g Fibre; 26 g Protein; 252 mg Sodium

Polenta-Topped Chili

*Smoky, hickory-flavoured chili gets even better with the addition of
unconventional polenta patties. Garnish with lime wedges, and add
Jicama Salad, page 22, for a marvelous Mexican-inspired meal!*

Cooking oil	2 tsp.	10 mL
Lean ground beef	1 lb.	454 g
Chopped onion	1 cup	250 mL
Garlic cloves, minced (or 1/2 tsp., 2 mL, powder)	2	2
Cans of black beans (19 oz., 540 mL, each), rinsed and drained	2	2
Can of crushed tomatoes	28 oz.	796 mL
Hickory barbecue sauce	1/4 cup	60 mL
Chili powder	2 tbsp.	30 mL
Seasoned salt	1/2 tsp.	2 mL
Polenta roll, cut into 12 slices	2.2 lbs.	1 kg
Grated jalapeño Monterey Jack cheese	1 cup	250 mL

Heat cooking oil in large frying pan on medium. Add next 3 ingredients.
Scramble-fry for about 10 minutes until beef is no longer pink.

Add next 5 ingredients. Stir. Bring to a boil. Transfer to ungreased
9 x 13 inch (22 x 33 cm) baking dish.

Arrange polenta on chili. Bake, uncovered, in 350°F (175°C) oven for about
20 minutes until polenta is heated through.

Sprinkle with cheese. Bake, uncovered, for another 10 to 12 minutes until
cheese is bubbling. Makes about 8 cups (2 L). Serves 6.

*1 serving: 672 Calories; 19.7 g Total Fat (7.4 g Mono, 1.7 g Poly, 8.2 g Sat); 62 mg Cholesterol;
86 g Carbohydrate; 16 g Fibre; 41 g Protein; 1000 mg Sodium*

Pictured on page 53.

Variation: For a different presentation, cut polenta into small cubes.
Scatter over top of chili.

Meatball And Potato Kabobs

About the easiest kabobs you can make, this meat(ball)
and potatoes meal-on-a-stick will be ready in no time.

Baby potatoes, halved	12	12
Cooking oil	1 tbsp.	15 mL
Italian seasoning	2 tsp.	10 mL
Frozen cooked meatballs, thawed	36	36
Pepper	1/4 tsp.	1 mL
Red pepper pieces (1 inch, 2.5 cm, size)	48	48
Bamboo skewers (8 inches, 20 cm, each), soaked in water for 10 minutes	12	12
Barbecue sauce	1/4 cup	60 mL

Put potato into medium microwave-safe bowl. Microwave on high (100%) for about 5 minutes until just tender.

Drizzle with cooking oil. Sprinkle with seasoning. Toss until coated. Set aside.

Put meatballs into large bowl. Sprinkle with pepper. Toss until coated.

Thread potato, meatballs and red pepper alternately onto skewers. Place kabobs on greased broiler pan.

Brush kabobs with barbecue sauce. Broil on centre rack in oven for 20 to 25 minutes, turning occasionally, until meatballs are heated through and potato is tender. Serves 4.

1 serving: 351 Calories; 18.8 g Total Fat (8.5 g Mono, 2.0 g Poly, 5.5 g Sat); 94 mg Cholesterol; 22 g Carbohydrate; 6 g Fibre; 23 g Protein; 310 mg Sodium

GRILLED MEATBALL AND POTATO KABOBS: Preheat gas barbecue to medium. Cook kabobs on greased grill for about 15 minutes, turning occasionally, until meatballs are heated through and potato is tender.

Satay Chicken Noodles

Sweet and spicy chicken takes a rest on a delicate bed of angel hair pasta.
Simply Thai-rrific with Asparagus Cucumber Salad, page 9.

Angel hair pasta, broken up	8 oz.	225 g
Sesame (or cooking) oil	1 tbsp.	15 mL
Water	1/4 cup	60 mL
Sweet chili sauce	2 tbsp.	30 mL
Chunky peanut butter	2 tbsp.	30 mL
Soy sauce	2 tbsp.	30 mL
Rice vinegar	1 tbsp.	15 mL
Cooking oil	1 tbsp.	15 mL
Boneless, skinless chicken breast halves, cut crosswise into 1/4 inch (6 mm) slices	1 lb.	454 g
Finely grated gingerroot (or 1/2 tsp., 2 mL, ground ginger)	2 tsp.	10 mL
Garlic clove, minced (or 1/4 tsp., 1 mL, powder)	1	1

Cook pasta in boiling salted water in large uncovered saucepan or Dutch oven for 6 to 8 minutes, stirring occasionally, until tender but firm. Drain. Transfer to large bowl.

Drizzle with sesame oil. Toss. Set aside.

Combine next 5 ingredients in small bowl.

Heat cooking oil in large frying pan on medium-high. Add remaining 3 ingredients. Cook for 3 to 5 minutes, stirring constantly, until chicken is no longer pink inside. Add peanut butter mixture. Heat and stir for 1 to 2 minutes until coated. Add pasta. Toss until heated through. Makes about 6 cups (1.5 L). Serves 4.

1 serving: 452 Calories; 13.6 g Total Fat (5.7 g Mono, 4.0 g Poly, 1.9 g Sat); 66 mg Cholesterol; 44 g Carbohydrate; 2 g Fibre; 36 g Protein; 762 mg Sodium

Hawaiian Burgers

Take a vacation from boring beef burgers with this
sweet and savoury chicken variation. Aloha!

Salad dressing (or mayonnaise)	2 tbsp.	30 mL
Thick teriyaki basting sauce	2 tbsp.	30 mL
Chicken breast cutlets	4	4
(4 – 6 oz., 113 – 170 g, each)		
Thick teriyaki basting sauce	1/4 cup	60 mL
Cooking oil	2 tsp.	10 mL
Deli ham slices (about 4 oz., 113 g)	4	4
Deli part-skim mozzarella cheese slices	4	4
(about 3 oz., 85 g)		
Canned pineapple slices, drained	4	4
Kaiser rolls, split	4	4
Lettuce leaves	8	8
Tomato slices	4	4

Combine salad dressing and first amount of teriyaki sauce in small cup. Set aside.

Brush both sides of chicken with second amount of teriyaki sauce. Heat oil in large frying pan on medium. Add chicken. Cook for about 4 minutes per side until no longer pink inside.

Place ham and cheese slices over chicken. Cook, covered, for 1 to 2 minutes until cheese is melted. Remove to large plate. Cover to keep warm.

Cook pineapple in same frying pan for about 1 minute per side until heated through and starting to brown.

Spread salad dressing mixture on rolls. Serve chicken, topped with pineapple, lettuce and tomato, in rolls. Serves 4.

1 serving: 527 Calories; 16.8 g Total Fat (6.7 g Mono, 4.1 g Poly, 4.2 g Sat); 94 mg Cholesterol; 49 g Carbohydrate; 2 g Fibre; 43 g Protein; 1517 mg Sodium

Sicilian Summer Grill

This tasty Italian treat may just be the grill of your dreams!
For a sensational supper in no time, start cooking the chicken
while you prepare the polenta and tomato. If your barbecue is
big enough, cook the polenta and tomato at the same time.

Boneless, skinless chicken thighs (about 3 oz., 85 g, each)	8	8
Seasoned salt	1 tsp.	5 mL
Pepper	1/2 tsp.	2 mL
Polenta roll, cut into 8 slices	1.1 lbs.	500 g
Basil pesto	1/4 cup	60 mL
Crumbled feta cheese (optional)	6 tbsp.	100 mL
Roma (plum) tomatoes, halved lengthwise	4	4
Olive (or cooking) oil	1 tbsp.	15 mL
Salt	1/4 tsp.	1 mL
Pepper	1/8 tsp.	0.5 mL

Sprinkle chicken with seasoned salt and first amount of pepper. Preheat gas barbecue to medium (see Tip, page 56). Cook chicken on greased grill for about 20 minutes, turning occasionally, until no longer pink inside. Remove to large serving plate. Cover to keep warm.

Brush both sides of polenta with pesto. Cook on greased grill for about 5 minutes until bottom is golden and grill marks appear. Turn polenta over.

Sprinkle with cheese. Cook for another 4 to 5 minutes until bottom is golden. Remove to same plate. Cover to keep warm.

Put tomato into medium bowl. Add olive oil. Sprinkle with salt and pepper. Toss gently until coated. Cook tomato, cut-side down, on greased grill for about 5 minutes until bottom starts to brown. Turn tomato over. Cook for another 4 to 5 minutes until slightly softened. Remove to same plate. Serves 4.

1 serving: 291 Calories; 12.3 g Total Fat (5.8 g Mono, 2.3 g Poly, 2.9 g Sat); 74 mg Cholesterol; 22 g Carbohydrate; 1 g Fibre; 23 g Protein; 568 mg Sodium

Pictured on page 35.

Island Chicken Casserole

*Forget the road—this chicken has gone clear across the Pacific
and returned loaded with tropical flavours. A meal in
itself, but even better with steamed rice.*

Red jalapeño jelly	1/2 cup	125 mL
Frozen concentrated orange juice	1/4 cup	60 mL
Thick teriyaki basting sauce	1/4 cup	60 mL
Garlic cloves, minced (or 1/2 tsp., 2 mL, powder)	2	2
Curry powder	1 tsp.	5 mL
Cubed peeled yam (or sweet potato)	3 cups	750 mL
Coarsely chopped onion	2 cups	500 mL
Can of pineapple chunks, drained	14 oz.	398 mL
Coarsely chopped green pepper	1 1/2 cups	375 mL
Bone-in chicken thighs (5 – 6 oz., 140 – 170 g, each)	8	8

Heat jelly in small saucepan on medium until melted. Remove from heat.

Add next 4 ingredients. Stir.

Put next 4 ingredients into greased 9 x 13 inch (22 x 33 cm) baking dish. Add 1/4 cup (60 mL) jelly mixture. Stir until coated.

Arrange chicken on vegetables. Spoon remaining jelly mixture onto chicken. Bake, uncovered, in 375°F (190°C) oven for about 1 hour until vegetables are tender and chicken is no longer pink inside. Serves 4.

1 serving: 674 Calories; 17.0 g Total Fat (6.3 g Mono, 4.0 g Poly, 4.7 g Sat); 143 mg Cholesterol; 87 g Carbohydrate; 8 g Fibre; 44 g Protein; 554 mg Sodium

Pictured on page 126.

Olive Chicken Bake

Olive lovers rejoice, a Greek feast awaits! Serve with steamed rice or potatoes for a complete meal.

Boneless, skinless chicken breast halves (4 – 6 oz., 113 – 170 g, each)	4	4
Diced eggplant (with peel)	2 cups	500 mL
Sun-dried tomato pesto	1/2 cup	125 mL
Chopped kalamata olives	1/2 cup	125 mL
Dried oregano	1 1/2 tsp.	7 mL
Garlic clove, minced (or 1/4 tsp., 1 mL, powder)	1	1
Pepper	1/2 tsp.	2 mL
Crumbled feta cheese	1/3 cup	75 mL

Put chicken into greased 2 quart (2 L) shallow baking dish.

Combine next 6 ingredients in medium bowl. Spoon onto chicken. Bake, uncovered, in 400°F (205°C) oven for about 30 minutes until chicken is no longer pink inside.

Sprinkle with cheese. Serves 4.

1 serving: 291 Calories; 12.9 g Total Fat (6.4 g Mono, 1.7 g Poly, 3.5 g Sat); 77 mg Cholesterol; 16 g Carbohydrate; 5 g Fibre; 31 g Protein; 471 mg Sodium

Crispy Chicken Drumettes

Backyard picnic anyone? Serve these crispy kid-pleasers with Herbed Potato Salad, page 13, and corn on the cob. Let the fun begin!

Salad dressing (or mayonnaise)	3/4 cup	175 mL
Chicken drumettes (or split chicken wings, tips discarded)	3 lbs.	1.4 kg
Crushed Ritz crackers (about 30)	1 cup	250 mL
Fine dry bread crumbs	3/4 cup	175 mL
Parsley flakes	2 tsp.	10 mL
Seasoned salt	2 tsp.	10 mL

(continued on next page)

Measure salad dressing into large bowl. Add chicken. Toss until coated.

Combine remaining 4 ingredients in small bowl. Put half of crumb mixture into large resealable freezer bag. Add half of chicken. Seal bag. Toss until coated. Arrange chicken on greased baking sheet with sides. Repeat with remaining crumb mixture and chicken. Discard any remaining crumb mixture. Bake in 375°F (190°C) oven for about 45 minutes until crumb coating is crisp and chicken is no longer pink inside. Makes about 24 drumettes (or 36 wing pieces). Serves 6.

1 serving: 619 Calories; 38.2 g Total Fat (17.6 g Mono, 11.1 g Poly, 6.6 g Sat); 193 mg Cholesterol; 19 g Carbohydrate; 1 g Fibre; 47 g Protein; 1075 mg Sodium

Pictured on page 72.

Curry-Spiced Chicken

Curry the favour of your household with this spicy and sweet marinated chicken. Terrific with fresh rolls and Minted Pea Salad, page 16, or Bulgur Vegetables, page 41.

Plain yogurt	1/2 cup	125 mL
Mango chutney, chopped	2 tbsp.	30 mL
Cooking oil	2 tbsp.	30 mL
Garam masala (see Tip, page 61)	1 tsp.	5 mL
Chili paste (sambal oelek)	1/2 tsp.	2 mL
Ground cumin	1/4 tsp.	1 mL
Turmeric	1/4 tsp.	1 mL
Salt	1/4 tsp.	1 mL
Boneless, skinless chicken breast halves (4 – 6 oz., 113 – 170 g, each)	4	4

Combine first 8 ingredients in small bowl.

Score top of chicken with sharp knife. Put into large resealable freezer bag. Add yogurt mixture. Seal bag. Turn until coated. Let stand in refrigerator for at least 6 hours or overnight, turning occasionally. Drain. Preheat gas barbecue to medium (see Tip, page 56). Place chicken on greased grill. Close lid. Cook for 6 to 8 minutes per side until chicken is no longer pink inside. Serves 4.

1 serving: 151 Calories; 3.8 g Total Fat (1.5 g Mono, 0.9 g Poly, 0.8 g Sat); 67 mg Cholesterol; 1 g Carbohydrate; trace Fibre; 26 g Protein; 104 mg Sodium

Pictured on page 17.

Chicken And Couscous

Opposites really do attract. Cooling mint and warming chili make a delightful pair in this easy recipe.

Cooking oil	1 tbsp.	15 mL
Boneless, skinless chicken breast halves, cut crosswise into thin slices (see Tip, page 87)	1 lb.	454 g
Chopped red onion	1 cup	250 mL
Chopped zucchini (with peel)	1 cup	250 mL
Grated carrot	1 cup	250 mL
Ground cumin	1 tsp.	5 mL
Dried crushed chilies	1/2 tsp.	2 mL
Montreal chicken spice	1/4 tsp.	1 mL
Pepper, sprinkle		
Prepared chicken broth	1 1/2 cups	375 mL
Orange juice	1/2 cup	125 mL
Frozen peas	1/2 cup	125 mL
Chopped fresh mint (or 3/4 tsp., 4 mL, dried)	1 tbsp.	15 mL
Grated orange zest	1 tsp.	5 mL
Plain couscous	1 cup	250 mL

Heat cooking oil in large frying pan on medium-high. Add chicken. Cook for about 5 minutes, stirring occasionally, until browned. Reduce heat to medium.

Add next 7 ingredients. Stir. Cook for about 5 minutes, stirring often, until onion starts to soften.

Add next 5 ingredients. Stir. Bring to a boil.

Add couscous. Stir. Remove from heat. Let stand, covered, for about 5 minutes until couscous is tender and broth is absorbed. Fluff with a fork. Makes about 6 cups (1.5 L). Serves 4.

1 serving: 410 Calories; 6.5 g Total Fat (2.8 g Mono, 1.8 g Poly, 1.0 g Sat); 66 mg Cholesterol; 50 g Carbohydrate; 5 g Fibre; 36 g Protein; 427 mg Sodium

Peanut Chicken Rice Bake

Working for peanuts isn't bad if you get to use them in dishes like this.
This easy and warming casserole will provide comfort to all. Serve
with Sweet Sugar Peas, page 62, for a crunchy contrast.

Prepared chicken broth	2 1/2 cups	625 mL
Long grain white rice	1 1/2 cups	375 mL
Cooking oil	1 tbsp.	15 mL
Garlic clove, minced (or 1/4 tsp., 1 mL, powder)	1	1
Boneless, skinless chicken thighs (about 3 oz., 85 g, each)	12	12
Diced onion	3/4 cup	175 mL
Diced red pepper	3/4 cup	175 mL
Peanut sauce	1 cup	250 mL

Combine first 4 ingredients in greased 9 x 13 inch (22 x 33 cm) baking dish.

Arrange chicken on rice mixture. Sprinkle with onion and red pepper.

Spoon peanut sauce over top. Bake, covered, in 375°F (190°C) oven for about 1 hour until rice is tender, broth is absorbed and chicken is no longer pink inside. Serves 6.

1 serving: 506 Calories; 22.0 g Total Fat (9.8 g Mono, 5.6 g Poly, 4.8 g Sat); 76 mg Cholesterol; 45 g Carbohydrate; 2 g Fibre; 32 g Protein; 486 mg Sodium

 tip To slice meat easily, before cutting place in freezer for about 30 minutes until just starting to freeze. If using from frozen state, partially thaw before cutting.

Lemon Herb Chicken

This subtly seasoned chicken is wonderful with Maple-Glazed Vegetables,
page 47. Marinate the chicken overnight if you like.

Olive (or cooking) oil	1/4 cup	60 mL
Liquid honey	1/4 cup	60 mL
Lemon juice	3 tbsp.	50 mL
Chopped fresh oregano (or 1 1/2 tsp., 7 mL, dried)	2 tbsp.	30 mL
Grated lemon zest	1 tbsp.	15 mL
Ground cumin	1 tbsp.	15 mL
Garlic cloves, minced (or 1/2 tsp., 2 mL, powder)	2	2
Salt	1/2 tsp.	2 mL
Chicken drumsticks (3 – 5 oz., 85 – 140 g, each)	12	12

Combine first 8 ingredients in small bowl. Reserve 3 tbsp. (50 mL) of olive
oil mixture in small cup for basting sauce.

Put chicken into large resealable freezer bag. Add remaining olive oil mixture.
Seal bag. Turn until coated. Let stand in refrigerator for 2 hours, turning
occasionally. Drain. Place chicken on greased wire rack set in foil-lined baking
sheet with sides. Bake in 375°F (190°C) oven for about 40 minutes, turning
occasionally and brushing with basting sauce, until no longer pink inside.
Serves 4.

1 serving: 499 Calories; 21.9 g Total Fat (8.7 g Mono, 4.7 g Poly, 5.1 g Sat); 262 mg Cholesterol;
6 g Carbohydrate; trace Fibre; 65 g Protein; 397 mg Sodium

1. Tortellini Chili Bake, page 68
2. Creamy Chicken Shrimp Penne, page 97

Props courtesy of: Casa Bugatti
                     Cherison Enterprises Inc.

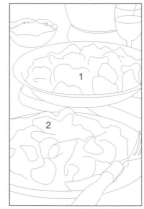

Tangy Chicken Potato Bake

*This mustard-flavoured chicken and potato dish is a must-have for
a great dinner. Serve with Sweet And Spicy Onions, page 58.*

Italian dressing	1/2 cup	125 mL
Honey Dijon mustard	1/4 cup	60 mL
Chopped fresh basil (or 1 1/2 tsp., 7 mL, dried)	2 tbsp.	30 mL
Boneless, skinless chicken breast halves (4 – 6 oz., 113 – 170 g, each)	4	4
Medium unpeeled potatoes, cut into 3/4 inch (2 cm) cubes	4	4
Salt, sprinkle		
Pepper, sprinkle		

Combine first 3 ingredients in small bowl. Reserve half of dressing mixture in small cup.

Put chicken into large resealable freezer bag. Add remaining dressing mixture. Seal bag. Turn until coated. Let stand in refrigerator for 2 hours. Drain.

Put potato into medium bowl. Add reserved dressing mixture, salt and pepper. Toss until coated. Arrange chicken breasts in centre of greased 9 x 13 inch (22 cm x 33 cm) baking dish. Arrange potato around chicken. Cover with foil. Cook in 375°F (190°C) oven for about 45 minutes until chicken is no longer pink inside and potato is tender. Serves 4.

1 serving: 297 Calories; 14.5 g Total Fat (7.5 g Mono, 4.6 g Poly, 1.4 g Sat); 78 mg Cholesterol; 12 g Carbohydrate; 8 g Fibre; 29 g Protein; 494 mg Sodium

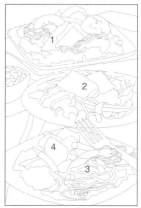

1. Grilled Beef Tomato Salad, page 24
2. Maple Miso Tofu Salad, page 32
3. Rice Noodle Salad, page 15
4. Grilled Chicken Kabobs, page 92

Props courtesy of: Stokes
Totally Bamboo

Zesty Chicken Kabobs

Savour the Asian flavour! Excellent with Rice Noodle Salad, page 15.

Soy sauce	1/4 cup	60 mL
Water	1/4 cup	60 mL
Brown sugar, packed	2 tbsp.	30 mL
Grated orange zest	2 tsp.	10 mL
Garlic cloves, minced (or 1/2 tsp., 2 mL, powder)	2	2
Finely grated gingerroot (or 1/4 tsp., 1 mL, ground ginger)	1 tsp.	5 mL
Pepper	1/2 tsp.	2 mL
Boneless, skinless chicken thighs, cut into 1 inch (2.5 cm) pieces	1 lb.	454 g
Green onions, cut into 1 inch (2.5 cm) pieces	6	6
Bamboo skewers (8 inches, 20 cm, each), soaked in water for 10 minutes	8	8

Combine first 7 ingredients in small bowl. Reserve half of soy sauce mixture in small cup for basting sauce.

Put chicken into medium resealable freezer bag. Add remaining soy sauce mixture. Seal bag. Turn until coated. Let stand in refrigerator for 30 minutes, turning occasionally. Drain.

Thread green onion and chicken alternately onto skewers, beginning and ending with green onion. Place kabobs on greased broiler pan. Brush with basting sauce. Broil on top rack in oven for 10 to 12 minutes, turning occasionally and brushing with any remaining basting sauce, until chicken is no longer pink inside. Serves 4.

1 serving: 231 Calories; 12.2 g Total Fat (4.8 g Mono, 2.7 g Poly, 3.4 g Sat); 73 mg Cholesterol; 9 g Carbohydrate; 1 g Fibre; 21 g Protein; 1058 mg Sodium

GRILLED CHICKEN KABOBS: Preheat gas barbecue to medium. Cook kabobs on greased grill for 10 to 12 minutes, turning occasionally and brushing with any remaining basting sauce, until chicken is no longer pink inside.

Pictured on page 90.

Baked Lemon Chicken

Tangy lemon enhances herbed chicken and vegetables.
An aromatic oven-baked meal that's sure to be a hit.

Olive (or cooking) oil	1 tbsp.	15 mL
Boneless, skinless chicken thighs (about 3 oz., 85 g, each)	12	12
Red baby potatoes, larger ones cut in half	1 1/2 lbs.	680 g
Small fresh whole white mushrooms	2 cups	500 mL
Small onion, cut into 8 wedges	1	1
Lemon juice	3 tbsp.	50 mL
Olive (or cooking) oil	3 tbsp.	50 mL
Water	3 tbsp.	50 mL
Grated lemon zest	1 tbsp.	15 mL
Dried oregano	2 1/2 tsp.	12 mL
Dried rosemary, crushed	1 tsp.	5 mL
Salt	1/2 tsp.	2 mL
Pepper	1/4 tsp.	1 mL
Baby carrots	2 cups	500 mL

Heat first amount of olive oil in large frying pan on medium-high. Add chicken. Cook for about 3 minutes per side until browned. Transfer to greased 3 quart (3 L) casserole.

Add next 3 ingredients.

Combine next 8 ingredients in small cup. Drizzle over chicken and vegetables. Toss until coated. Bake, uncovered, in 400°F (205°C) oven for 20 minutes.

Add carrots. Bake, covered, for another 25 to 30 minutes until chicken is no longer pink inside and carrots are tender-crisp. Serves 6.

1 serving: 360 Calories; 17.8 g Total Fat (9.9 g Mono, 2.8 g Poly, 3.7 g Sat); 74 mg Cholesterol; 26 g Carbohydrate; 4 g Fibre; 24 g Protein; 294 mg Sodium

Confetti Rice And Chicken

Time to celebrate the little dining pleasures in life—we've even included the confetti! Tender chicken atop rice with festive flecks of cranberry and vegetables is certain to get the party started.

Boneless, skinless chicken thighs (about 3 oz., 85 g, each)	8	8
Seasoned salt	1/2 tsp.	2 mL
Pepper	1/4 tsp.	1 mL
Cooking oil	1 tbsp.	15 mL
Prepared chicken broth	2 cups	500 mL
Grated peeled yam (or sweet potato)	1 1/2 cups	375 mL
Converted white rice	1 cup	250 mL
Grated carrot	1 cup	250 mL
Dried cranberries	3/4 cup	175 mL
Finely chopped onion	1/2 cup	125 mL
Butter (or hard margarine), melted	1 tbsp.	15 mL
Dried thyme	1 tsp.	5 mL

Sprinkle chicken with seasoned salt and pepper.

Heat cooking oil in large frying pan on medium-high. Add chicken. Cook for about 5 minutes per side until browned. Remove from heat.

Combine remaining 8 ingredients in ungreased 2 quart (2 L) casserole. Arrange chicken on rice mixture. Bake, covered, in 350°F (175°C) oven for about 1 hour until rice is tender and broth is absorbed. Serves 4.

1 serving: 569 Calories; 16.5 g Total Fat (6.5 g Mono, 3.6 g Poly, 4.8 g Sat); 82 mg Cholesterol; 77 g Carbohydrate; 6 g Fibre; 28 g Protein; 679 mg Sodium

Chicken Tortilla Bake

A saucy casserole with southwestern flair. Make
it a fiesta with Corn-Stuffed Tomatoes, page 42.

Diced cooked chicken	1 1/2 cups	375 mL
Can of condensed cream of mushroom soup	10 oz.	284 mL
Chopped onion	1 cup	250 mL
Milk	2/3 cup	150 mL
Can of diced green chilies	4 oz.	113 g
Corn tortillas (6 inch, 15 cm, diameter), each cut into 4 wedges	6	6
Grated medium Cheddar cheese	1 1/2 cups	375 mL

Combine first 5 ingredients in medium bowl.

Arrange half of tortilla wedges in greased 2 quart (2 L) casserole. Layer with half of chicken mixture.

Sprinkle with half of cheese. Repeat with remaining ingredients. Bake, uncovered, in 350°F (175°C) oven for about 50 minutes until heated through and cheese is bubbling. Serves 6.

1 serving: 301 Calories; 15.9 g Total Fat (3.8 g Mono, 1.2 g Poly, 7.9 g Sat); 61 mg Cholesterol; 20 g Carbohydrate; 3 g Fibre; 20 g Protein; 651 mg Sodium

---

Paré Pointer
No wonder their coffee tastes like mud. It was ground ten minutes ago.

Jiffy Jambalaya

Spice up dinner tonight with this traditional Cajun meal and laissez les bons temps rouler (let the good times roll). Smoky sausage and tender chicken flavour this mildly-spiced jambalaya blend.

Cooking oil	1 tbsp.	15 mL
Chopped celery	1 cup	250 mL
Chopped onion	1 cup	250 mL
Chopped green pepper	1 cup	250 mL
Smoked ham sausage, cut into 1/2 inch (12 mm) slices	5 oz.	140 g
Can of diced tomatoes (with juice)	14 oz.	398 mL
Prepared chicken broth	1 1/2 cups	375 mL
Long grain white rice	1 1/4 cups	300 mL
Cajun seasoning	1 tbsp.	15 mL
Cayenne pepper	1/2 tsp.	2 mL
Precooked whole roasted chicken (see Note)	2 1/2 – 3 lbs.	1.1 – 1.4 kg

Chopped fresh parsley, for garnish

Heat cooking oil in large saucepan or Dutch oven on medium-high. Add next 4 ingredients. Cook for 5 to 10 minutes, stirring occasionally, until vegetables start to soften and sausage is heated through.

Add next 5 ingredients. Stir. Bring to a boil. Reduce heat to medium-low. Simmer, covered, for about 20 minutes, without stirring, until rice is tender and liquid is absorbed. Let stand for 5 minutes. Fluff with a fork.

Remove chicken from bones. Chop coarsely. Add to rice mixture. Stir. Remove to large serving dish.

Garnish with parsley. Makes about 9 cups (2.4 L). Serves 6.

1 serving: 608 Calories; 23.0 g Total Fat (9.8 g Mono, 4.6 g Poly, 6.5 g Sat); 158 mg Cholesterol; 39 g Carbohydrate; 2 g Fibre; 58 g Protein; 1160 mg Sodium

Pictured on page 125.

Note: If you have leftover cooked chicken, use 4 cups (1 L) chopped cooked chicken in place of the precooked whole roasted chicken.

Creamy Chicken Shrimp Penne

A penne for your thoughts? Pile chicken, shrimp, spinach and tomatoes
on top of penne and we know what you'll be thinking—simply delicious!

Penne pasta	4 cups	1 L
Olive (or cooking) oil	2 tsp.	10 mL
Boneless, skinless chicken breast halves, cut crosswise into slices	1 lb.	454 g
Garlic cloves, minced (or 1/2 tsp., 2 mL, powder)	2	2
Dry (or alcohol-free) white wine	1/4 cup	60 mL
Can of evaporated milk	13 1/2 oz.	385 mL
Salt	1/2 tsp.	2 mL
Cayenne pepper	1/4 tsp.	1 mL
Frozen, uncooked medium shrimp (peeled and deveined), thawed	1/2 lb.	225 g
Chopped fresh spinach, lightly packed	1 cup	250 mL
Grated Parmesan cheese	1/2 cup	125 mL
Roma (plum) tomatoes, chopped	3	3

Cook pasta in boiling salted water in large uncovered saucepan or Dutch oven for 8 to 10 minutes, stirring occasionally, until tender but firm. Drain. Return to same saucepan. Cover to keep warm.

Heat olive oil in large frying pan on medium. Add chicken and garlic. Cook for 5 to 10 minutes, stirring occasionally, until chicken is no longer pink inside and starts to brown. Add to pasta. Toss. Cover to keep warm.

Add wine to same frying pan. Heat and stir, scraping any brown bits from bottom of pan. Bring to a boil. Reduce heat to medium. Boil gently for about 1 minute until reduced by half.

Add next 3 ingredients. Stir. Boil gently for 5 minutes, stirring often.

Add shrimp. Stir. Cook, uncovered, for about 3 minutes until shrimp turn pink.

Add remaining 3 ingredients. Heat and stir for about 1 minute until spinach is wilted. Add to pasta mixture. Toss. Makes about 10 1/2 cups (2.6 L). Serves 4.

1 serving: 625 Calories; 17.4 g Total Fat (5.7 g Mono, 1.4 g Poly, 7.9 g Sat); 190 mg Cholesterol; 54 g Carbohydrate; 2 g Fibre; 57 g Protein; 782 mg Sodium

Pictured on page 89.

Curried Tuna Quiche

It's not a silly notion at all! Fusilli pasta adds an attractive and unusual touch to traditional quiche. Serve with a green salad. To lighten your work, use a pre-grated mozzarella and Cheddar cheese blend.

Pastry for 9 inch (22 cm) pie shell

Cooked fusilli pasta (about 2/3 cup, 150 mL, uncooked)	1 cup	250 mL
Grated zucchini (with peel), squeezed dry	1 cup	250 mL
Can of flaked white tuna in water, drained	6 oz.	170 g
Grated mozzarella cheese	1/2 cup	125 mL
Grated medium Cheddar cheese	1/2 cup	125 mL
Large eggs	3	3
All-purpose flour	1 tbsp.	15 mL
Curry powder	1 tsp.	5 mL
Salt	1/2 tsp.	2 mL
Pepper	1/4 tsp.	1 mL
Skim evaporated milk	1 1/4 cups	300 mL
Roma (plum) tomatoes, sliced	2	2

Roll out pastry on lightly floured surface to 1/8 inch (3 mm) thickness. Line 9 inch (22 cm) pie plate. Trim and crimp decorative edge.

Scatter next 5 ingredients in pie shell. Set aside.

Beat next 5 ingredients in medium bowl until smooth.

Add evaporated milk. Stir. Pour into pie shell.

Top with tomato. Bake on bottom rack in 350°F (175°C) oven for 60 to 65 minutes until knife inserted in centre comes out clean. Let stand for 10 minutes. Serves 6.

1 serving: 388 Calories; 19.6 g Total Fat (2.9 g Mono, 0.9 g Poly, 7.1 g Sat); 124 mg Cholesterol; 30 g Carbohydrate; 1 g Fibre; 21 g Protein; 566 mg Sodium

Pictured on page 54.

Balsamic Skewers

*A delicious basting sauce is only a bottle of balsamic vinaigrette away—
perfect for succulent shrimp. Use thick-stalked asparagus in this recipe
for best results on the grill. Cajun Cheese Bread, page 40, or
Dill Pasta Salad, page 19, will finish this meal nicely.*

Frozen, uncooked large shrimp (peeled and deveined), thawed	1 lb.	454 g
Bamboo skewers (8 inches, 20 cm, each), soaked in water for 10 minutes	8	8
Can of whole baby corn, drained and cut into 1 inch (2.5 cm) pieces	14 oz.	398 mL
Fresh asparagus, trimmed of tough ends and cut into 1 inch (2.5 cm) pieces	3/4 lb.	340 g
Green onions (white parts only), cut into 1 inch (2.5 cm) pieces	6	6
Large red pepper, cut into 1 inch (2.5 cm) pieces	1	1
Bamboo skewers (8 inches, 20 cm, each), soaked in water for 10 minutes	8	8
Balsamic vinaigrette	1/2 cup	125 mL

Thread shrimp onto first 8 skewers (see Note). Place skewers on ungreased baking sheet with sides.

Thread next 4 ingredients alternately onto next 8 skewers. Place on same baking sheet.

Brush skewers with vinaigrette. Preheat gas barbecue to medium (see Tip, page 56). Cook vegetable skewers on greased grill for about 8 minutes, turning once at halftime, until vegetables are tender-crisp. Cook shrimp skewers on greased grill for about 2 minutes per side until shrimp turn pink. Serves 4.

1 serving: 355 Calories; 11.6 g Total Fat (0.7 g Mono, 1.5 g Poly, 1.6 g Sat); 172 mg Cholesterol; 38 g Carbohydrate; 5 g Fibre; 29 g Protein; 491 mg Sodium

Note: Thread shrimp body and tail through the skewers to ensure even cooking.

Pictured on page 18.

Salmon French Loaf

*Say bonjour to this warm take on the classic salmon salad sandwich.
It's just as good baked in the oven or served cold. Serve with your
favourite pickles and Walnut Green Salad, page 12.*

Cans of red (or pink) salmon (7 1/2 oz., 213 g, each), drained, skin and round bones removed	2	2
Block of cream cheese, softened	8 oz.	250 g
Roasted red peppers, blotted dry and diced	1/2 cup	125 mL
Green onions, sliced	2	2
Grated lemon zest	1 tsp.	5 mL
Pepper	1 tsp.	5 mL
French bread loaf, halved lengthwise	1	1

Combine first 6 ingredients in large bowl.

Spread salmon mixture on bottom half of loaf. Cover with top half.
Secure with 6 wooden picks evenly spaced apart. Wrap tightly in sheet of
heavy-duty (or double layer of regular) foil. Bake in 375°F (190°C) oven for
20 to 30 minutes until heated through. Cut crosswise between wooden
picks into 6 pieces. Serves 6.

*1 serving: 476 Calories; 23.2 g Total Fat (4.6 g Mono, 1.0 g Poly, 10.5 g Sat); 87 mg Cholesterol;
42 g Carbohydrate; 2 g Fibre; 25 g Protein; 1037 mg Sodium*

Feta Shrimp Frittata

*This delightful frittata makes a nice, light meal when served
with Fresh Herb Rice, page 43, and your favourite salad.*

Cooking oil	1 tbsp.	15 mL
Chopped green pepper	1 cup	250 mL
Chopped onion	1/4 cup	60 mL
Large eggs	8	8
Herb and garlic cream cheese	1/4 cup	60 mL
Cooked salad shrimp	3/4 lb.	340 g
Crumbled feta cheese	1 cup	250 mL
Pepper	1/2 tsp.	2 mL

(continued on next page)

Heat cooking oil in large frying pan on medium. Add green pepper and onion. Cook for 5 to 10 minutes, stirring often, until vegetables are softened.

Beat eggs and cream cheese in medium bowl until smooth. Add remaining 3 ingredients. Stir. Pour over vegetables in frying pan. Stir for 5 seconds. Spread egg mixture evenly in pan. Reduce heat to medium-low. Cook, covered, for about 10 minutes until bottom is golden and top is almost set. Broil on centre rack in oven (see Tip, page 115) for 2 to 3 minutes until frittata is golden and set. Serves 4.

1 serving: 456 Calories; 33.0 g Total Fat (10.2 g Mono, 6.7 g Poly, 12.6 g Sat); 518 mg Cholesterol; 8 g Carbohydrate; 1 g Fibre; 31 g Protein; 806 mg Sodium

---

Orzo Shrimp Packets

Pasta on the barbecue? You bet! You'll love this flavourful shrimp and orzo combination.

Chopped tomato	2 cups	500 mL
Sliced leek (white part only)	1 cup	250 mL
Dry (or alcohol-free) white wine	1/4 cup	60 mL
Olive (or cooking) oil	1 tbsp.	15 mL
Parsley flakes	1 tbsp.	15 mL
Garlic cloves, minced (or 3/4 tsp., 4 mL, powder)	3	3
Salt	1/2 tsp.	2 mL
Granulated sugar	1/4 tsp.	1 mL
Cooked orzo (about 1 1/2 cups, 375 mL, uncooked)	3 cups	750 mL
Frozen, uncooked medium shrimp (peeled and deveined), thawed	1 lb.	454 g

Combine first 8 ingredients in large bowl.

Add orzo and shrimp. Stir. Transfer to four greased sheets of heavy-duty (or double layer of regular) foil. Fold edges of foil together over shrimp mixture to enclose. Fold ends to seal completely. Preheat gas barbecue to medium. Place packets on ungreased grill. Close lid. Cook for about 15 minutes, turning once at halftime, until shrimp turn pink. Serves 4.

1 serving: 451 Calories; 6.6 g Total Fat (2.8 g Mono, 1.2 g Poly, 1.2 g Sat); 172 mg Cholesterol; 61 g Carbohydrate; 4 g Fibre; 34 g Protein; 475 mg Sodium

Tarragon Shrimp Linguine

*Dahling! Dinner is simply divine when tarragon and
white wine accent a buttery shrimp-and-pasta toss.*

Linguine	12 oz.	340 g
Cooking oil	1 tbsp.	15 mL
Frozen, uncooked large shrimp (peeled and deveined), thawed	1 lb.	454 g
Julienned carrot (see Tip, page 140)	2 cups	500 mL
Prepared chicken broth	1 cup	250 mL
Dry (or alcohol-free) white wine	1/3 cup	75 mL
Lemon juice	1 tbsp.	15 mL
Chopped fresh tarragon (or 1/4 tsp., 1 mL, dried)	1 tsp.	5 mL
Water	2 tbsp.	30 mL
Cornstarch	2 tsp.	10 mL
Chopped fresh chives	1/4 cup	60 mL
Butter (or hard margarine)	1 tbsp.	15 mL

Cook pasta in boiling salted water in large uncovered saucepan or Dutch
oven for 8 to 10 minutes, stirring occasionally, until tender but firm. Drain.
Return to same saucepan. Cover to keep warm.

Heat cooking oil in large frying pan on medium-high. Add shrimp. Heat
and stir for 2 to 3 minutes until shrimp turn pink. Transfer to small bowl.
Set aside.

Combine next 5 ingredients in same frying pan. Bring to a boil. Reduce heat
to medium. Cook, covered, for about 3 minutes until carrot is tender-crisp.

Stir water into cornstarch in small cup. Stir into carrot mixture. Add shrimp.
Heat and stir for about 1 minute until sauce is boiling and thickened and
shrimp are heated through. Remove from heat.

Add chives and butter. Heat and stir until butter is melted. Add to pasta.
Toss. Makes about 7 cups (1.75 L). Serves 4.

*1 serving: 542 Calories; 9.9 g Total Fat (3.2 g Mono, 2.0 g Poly, 2.9 g Sat); 180 mg Cholesterol;
73 g Carbohydrate; 4 g Fibre; 37 g Protein; 429 mg Sodium*

Scallop "Orzotto"

Our pasta version of risotto. Made with orzo, tiny rice-shaped pasta, this dish is rich, creamy and loaded with scallops and mushrooms. Lemon Pepper Greens, page 59, will add a delightful splash of colour to this meal.

Orzo	2 cups	500 mL
Garlic butter	1 tbsp.	15 mL
Sliced fresh white mushrooms	1 1/2 cups	375 mL
Prepared chicken broth	1 1/2 cups	375 mL
Grated lemon zest	1/2 tsp.	2 mL
Dried oregano	1/4 tsp.	1 mL
Fresh (or frozen, thawed) small bay scallops	2 cups	500 mL
Grated Parmesan cheese	1/2 cup	125 mL
Garlic butter	1 tbsp.	15 mL
Lemon juice	1 tbsp.	15 mL
Pepper	1/4 tsp.	1 mL

Cook orzo in boiling salted water in large uncovered saucepan or Dutch oven for about 5 minutes, stirring occasionally, until almost tender. Drain. Rinse with cold water. Drain well. Set aside.

Melt first amount of garlic butter in same saucepan on medium. Add mushrooms. Cook for about 5 minutes, stirring occasionally, until softened.

Add orzo and next 3 ingredients. Stir. Bring to a boil. Reduce heat to medium-low. Simmer, uncovered, for 5 minutes, stirring constantly.

Add scallops. Heat and stir for about 5 minutes until scallops are opaque and broth is absorbed.

Add remaining 4 ingredients. Heat and stir until butter is melted. Makes about 6 1/2 cups (1.6 L). Serves 4.

1 serving: 538 Calories; 11.9 g Total Fat (1.4 g Mono, 0.5 g Poly, 5.5 g Sat); 57 mg Cholesterol; 68 g Carbohydrate; 3 g Fibre; 38 g Protein; 767 mg Sodium

Asian Salmon Burgers

This Asian-inspired dish will go over swimmingly! Top with lettuce, tomato and add Asparagus Cucumber Salad, page 9, on the side.

Mayonnaise	2 tbsp.	30 mL
Chopped pickled ginger	1 tbsp.	15 mL
Wasabi paste (Japanese horseradish)	1/2 tsp.	2 mL
Large egg, fork-beaten	1	1
Finely chopped green onion	1/4 cup	60 mL
Soy sauce	1 tbsp.	15 mL
Finely grated gingerroot (or 1/4 tsp., 1 mL, ground ginger)	1 1/2 tsp.	7 mL
Honey Dijon mustard	1 tsp.	5 mL
Fresh (or frozen, thawed) salmon fillet, skin and any small bones removed, coarsely chopped	1 lb.	454 g
Fine dry bread crumbs	1/2 cup	125 mL
Onion buns, split	4	4

Combine first 3 ingredients in small cup. Chill.

Combine next 5 ingredients in medium bowl. Set aside.

Put fish into food processor. Process with on/off motion until finely chopped.

Add bread crumbs. Process with on/off motion until combined. Add to egg mixture. Mix well. Divide into 4 equal portions. Shape into 4 inch (10 cm) diameter patties. Place on greased broiler pan. Broil on top rack in oven for about 5 minutes per side until golden and set. Remove to large plate. Cover to keep warm.

Place buns cut-side up on same broiler pan. Broil on top rack in oven for 1 to 2 minutes until golden. Serve patties, topped with mayonnaise mixture, in buns. Serves 4.

1 serving: 512 Calories; 17.7 g Total Fat (6.3 g Mono, 5.1 g Poly, 3.2 g Sat); 123 mg Cholesterol; 51 g Carbohydrate; 3 g Fibre; 34 g Protein; 1155 mg Sodium

GRILLED SALMON BURGERS: Preheat gas barbecue to medium. Cook patties on greased grill for about 5 minutes per side until golden and set. Toast buns cut-side down on greased grill. Serve grilled patties, topped with mayonnaise mixture, in buns.

Pictured on page 107.

Salmon Polenta Skewers

Polenta, ham-wrapped salmon and tender-crisp vegetables make quite an eye-catching meal. But don't fret, this is easy. You'll have dinner on the table faster than you can say "kabob's your uncle!" Serve with grilled vegetables or salad.

Italian dressing	1/4 cup	60 mL
Sun-dried tomato pesto	1 tbsp.	15 mL
Deli ham slices, each cut into 4 strips (about 1 inch, 2.5 cm, wide)	4	4
Fresh (or frozen, thawed) salmon fillet, skin removed, cut into 1 1/2 inch (3.8 cm) cubes	1 lb.	454 g
Zucchini slices (with peel), cut 1 inch, 2.5 cm, thick, halved crosswise	8	8
Polenta cubes (1 inch, 2.5 cm, size)	16	16
Red pepper pieces (1 inch, 2.5 cm, size)	16	16
Bamboo skewers (8 inches, 20 cm, each), soaked in water for 10 minutes	8	8

Combine dressing and pesto in small cup. Set aside.

Wrap ham strips around fish pieces.

Thread fish and next 3 ingredients alternately onto skewers. Place on large plate. Brush skewers with pesto mixture. Preheat gas barbecue to medium (see Tip, page 56). Cook skewers on greased grill for 10 to 12 minutes, turning occasionally, until vegetables are tender-crisp and fish flakes easily when tested with a fork. Serves 4.

1 serving: 421 Calories; 19.5 g Total Fat (8.5 g Mono, 6.4 g Poly, 2.0 g Sat); 112 mg Cholesterol; 21 g Carbohydrate; 1 g Fibre; 41 g Protein; 1520 mg Sodium

Pictured on page 107.

Paré Pointer
He tried to book a trip to the moon but it was already full.

Dijon Dill Salmon Patties

Salmon patties are made simply sensational when paired with Dijon mustard and dill. A perfect match for Vegetable Pearl Salad, page 14.

Large eggs, fork-beaten	2	2
Crushed Ritz crackers (about 24)	3/4 cup	175 mL
Finely chopped green onion	1/2 cup	125 mL
Honey Dijon mustard	2 tbsp.	30 mL
Chopped fresh dill (or 1 1/2 tsp., 7 mL, dried)	2 tbsp.	30 mL
Grated lemon zest	2 tsp.	10 mL
Cans of pink salmon (6 1/2 oz., 184 g, each), drained, skin and round bones removed	4	4
Cooking oil	2 tbsp.	30 mL
Lemon wedges, for garnish		

Combine first 6 ingredients in medium bowl.

Add salmon. Mix well. Divide into 6 equal portions. Shape into 4 inch (10 cm) diameter patties.

Heat 1 tbsp. (15 mL) cooking oil in large frying pan on medium. Add 3 patties. Cook for about 3 minutes per side until golden. Remove to large serving plate. Cover to keep warm. Repeat with remaining cooking oil and patties.

Garnish with lemon wedges. Serves 6.

1 serving: 281 Calories; 13.6 g Total Fat (4.5 g Mono, 2.2 g Poly, 2.0 g Sat); 151 mg Cholesterol; 8 g Carbohydrate; 1 g Fibre; 34 g Protein; 688 mg Sodium

1. Smoky Asparagus Salad, page 9
2. Grilled Salmon Burgers, page 104
3. Salmon Polenta Skewers, page 105

Props courtesy of: Cherison Enterprises Inc.
Emile Henry

Nacho-Crusted Haddock

Definitely nacho ordinary fish sticks! Serve alongside Vegetable Spanish Rice, page 51, for a meal the whole family will love.

Haddock fillets, any small bones removed, cut into 6 equal pieces	1 1/2 lbs.	680 g
Mayonnaise	2 tbsp.	30 mL
Finely chopped cilantro or parsley (or 3/4 tsp., 4 mL, dried)	1 tbsp.	15 mL
Crushed cheese-flavoured tortilla chips	1 cup	250 mL
Grated medium Cheddar cheese	1/3 cup	75 mL
Lime juice	1 tbsp.	15 mL
Grated lime zest	1/2 tsp.	2 mL

Arrange fish on greased foil-lined baking sheet with sides.

Combine mayonnaise and cilantro in small cup. Spread on fish.

Combine remaining 4 ingredients in small bowl. Spoon onto fish. Press down lightly with back of spoon. Bake in 375°F (190°C) oven for 8 to 10 minutes until fish flakes easily when tested with a fork. Serves 6.

1 serving: 281 Calories; 12.9 g Total Fat (6.5 g Mono, 2.4 g Poly, 3.0 g Sat); 74 mg Cholesterol; 16 g Carbohydrate; 1 g Fibre; 25 g Protein; 314 mg Sodium

Pictured at left.

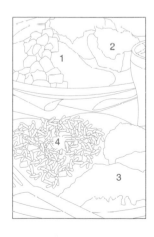

1. Grilled Salmon With Avocado Salsa, page 110
2. Grilled Chipotle Cheese Potatoes, page 52
3. Nacho-Crusted Haddock, above
4. Vegetable Spanish Rice, page 51

Props courtesy of: Pfaltzgraff Canada
Stokes

Salmon With Avocado Salsa

Forget the guacamole, avocado salsa is where it's at. Chunks of avocado and cucumber atop lemon pepper salmon will have you feeling cool on those hot summer nights. Nicely complemented by Chipotle Cheese Potatoes, page 52.

Fresh (or frozen, thawed) salmon fillets (about 4 oz., 113 g, each), skin removed	4	4
Lemon pepper	1 tsp.	5 mL
CUCUMBER AVOCADO SALSA		
English cucumber (with peel), seeds removed, diced	1 1/2 cups	375 mL
Ripe medium avocado, chopped	1	1
Lime juice	1/3 cup	75 mL
Chopped red onion	1/4 cup	60 mL
Chopped fresh cilantro or parsley	1/4 cup	60 mL
Liquid honey	1 tbsp.	15 mL
Finely chopped fresh jalapeño pepper (see Tip, below)	1 tsp.	5 mL

Sprinkle fish with lemon pepper. Place on greased broiler pan. Broil on top rack in oven for 2 to 4 minutes per side, depending on thickness, until fish flakes easily when tested with a fork.

Cucumber Avocado Salsa: Combine all 7 ingredients in medium bowl. Makes about 2 1/2 cups (625 mL) salsa. Serve with fish. Serves 4.

1 serving: 257 Calories; 14.8 g Total Fat (2.4 g Mono, 2.9 g Poly, 1.8 g Sat); 62 mg Cholesterol; 11 g Carbohydrate; 2 g Fibre; 24 g Protein; 84 mg Sodium

GRILLED SALMON WITH AVOCADO SALSA: Preheat gas barbecue to medium-high. Cook fish on greased grill for 2 to 4 minutes per side, depending on thickness, until fish flakes easily when tested with a fork.

Pictured on page 108.

 tip Hot peppers contain capsaicin in the seeds and ribs. Removing the seeds and ribs will reduce the heat. Wear rubber gloves when handling hot peppers and avoid touching your eyes. Wash your hands well afterwards.

Artichoke Salmon

Artichoke is always an artful choice when it comes to impressing guests. They'll be full of accolades when they taste the smoky bacon and artichoke stuffing atop sensational salmon. Serve with wild rice and Braised Celery, page 48.

Bacon slices, diced	2	2
Sliced fresh white mushrooms	2 cups	500 mL
Chopped onion	1/2 cup	125 mL
Large egg, fork-beaten	1	1
Seasoned croutons	1 1/2 cups	375 mL
Jar of marinated artichoke hearts, drained and chopped	6 oz.	170 mL
Prepared chicken broth	1/4 cup	60 mL
Grated Parmesan cheese	1/4 cup	60 mL
Fresh (or frozen, thawed) salmon fillet, with skin, any small bones removed	2 lbs.	900 g

Cook bacon in large frying pan on medium until crisp.

Add mushrooms and onion. Cook for 5 to 10 minutes, stirring often, until onion is softened. Transfer to large bowl.

Add next 5 ingredients. Stir until croutons are moistened.

Place fish, skin-side down, on greased baking sheet. Spoon crouton mixture on top. Press down lightly with back of spoon. Bake in 375°F (190°C) oven for about 20 minutes until fish flakes easily when tested with a fork. Serves 6.

1 serving: 341 Calories; 16.0 g Total Fat (5.3 g Mono, 4.4 g Poly, 3.4 g Sat); 120 mg Cholesterol; 12 g Carbohydrate; 2 g Fibre; 37 g Protein; 467 mg Sodium

---

Paré Pointer
How come a lawyer writes a 90 page document and calls it a brief?

Shrimp Fried Rice

*Got rice? If you have leftover rice in the fridge, you can have dinner
on the table in minutes (results are better if the rice is cold).
Serve with steamed sugar snap peas on the side.*

Cooking oil	1 tbsp.	15 mL
Sliced celery	1/2 cup	125 mL
Garlic clove, minced (or 1/4 tsp., 1 mL, powder)	1	1
Finely grated gingerroot (or 1/8 tsp., 0.5 mL, ground ginger)	1/2 tsp.	2 mL
Cooking oil	1 tbsp.	15 mL
Large eggs	4	4
Pepper, sprinkle		
Cooked long grain white rice (about 1 1/3 cups, 325 mL, uncooked)	4 cups	1 L
Sliced green onion	1 cup	250 mL
Soy sauce	2 tbsp.	30 mL
Cooked baby shrimp	1 lb.	454 g
Frozen peas, thawed	1 cup	250 mL

Heat wok or large frying pan on medium-high until very hot. Add first
amount of cooking oil. Add next 3 ingredients. Stir-fry for about 1 minute
until celery is softened. Transfer to small bowl. Set aside.

Add second amount of cooking oil to hot wok. Break eggs into wok.
Sprinkle with pepper. Break yolks. Cook for 1 to 2 minutes until eggs start
to set. Turn eggs over. Stir-fry for 1 to 2 minutes until egg starts to brown.

Add next 3 ingredients. Stir-fry for about 5 minutes until rice starts to brown.

Add celery mixture, shrimp and peas. Stir-fry for about 3 minutes until
heated through. Makes about 8 cups (2 L). Serves 4.

*1 serving: 503 Calories; 14.4 g Total Fat (6.6 g Mono, 3.7 g Poly, 2.6 g Sat); 359 mg Cholesterol;
54 g Carbohydrate; 3 g Fibre; 37 g Protein; 944 mg Sodium*

Sole Packets

*The pirate in you will take great delight in this buried treasure
of tender sole hidden under fragrant coconut and curry couscous.*

Sole fillets, any small bones removed, divided into 4 equal portions	1 lb.	454 g
Salt	1/4 tsp.	1 mL
Pepper	1/8 tsp.	0.5 mL
Prepared chicken broth	1 cup	250 mL
Coconut milk (or reconstituted from powder)	1/2 cup	125 mL
Granulated sugar	2 tbsp.	30 mL
Curry powder	1 tbsp.	15 mL
Finely grated gingerroot (or 1/2 tsp., 2 mL, ground ginger)	2 tsp.	10 mL
Parsley flakes	2 tsp.	10 mL
Salt	1/4 tsp.	1 mL
Frozen peas	2 cups	500 mL
Plain couscous	1 1/2 cups	375 mL

Sprinkle fish with first amount of salt and pepper. Place on 4 greased sheets of heavy-duty (or double layer of regular) foil. Set aside.

Combine next 7 ingredients in large bowl.

Add peas and couscous. Stir. Spoon onto fish. Fold edges of foil together over couscous mixture to enclose. Fold ends to seal completely. Preheat gas barbecue to medium. Place packets on ungreased grill. Close lid. Cook for 15 to 20 minutes, turning once at halftime, until fish flakes easily when tested with a fork. Serves 4.

1 serving: 516 Calories; 9.0 g Total Fat (0.9 g Mono, 0.9 g Poly, 6.3 g Sat); 54 mg Cholesterol; 72 g Carbohydrate; 6 g Fibre; 36 g Protein; 671 mg Sodium

Oven Salmon Scallop

*To the table they'll gallop for a taste of this scallop! Salmon,
potatoes and vegetables are smothered in a creamy
sauce—especially nice on a cold, blustery day!*

Thinly sliced peeled potato (about 1 1/2 lbs., 680 g)	4 cups	1 L
Thinly sliced carrot	1 cup	250 mL
Thinly sliced onion	1 cup	250 mL
Thinly sliced celery	3/4 cup	175 mL
Fresh (or frozen, thawed) salmon fillets, skin removed, cut into 1 inch (2.5 cm) pieces	1 lb.	454 g
Milk	2 cups	500 mL
Envelope of leek soup mix	2 3/4 oz.	77 g

Layer half of first 4 ingredients, in order given, in greased 9 × 13 inch
(22 × 33 cm) baking dish.

Arrange fish on celery. Layer remaining vegetables on top. Set aside.

Heat milk in small saucepan on medium until hot but not boiling. Slowly
add soup mix, stirring constantly until thickened. Pour over vegetables,
poking with knife in several places to bottom of baking dish to allow soup
mixture to flow through. Bake, covered, in 350°F (175°C) oven for about
1 hour until vegetables are tender and fish flakes easily when tested with
a fork. Serves 4.

*1 serving: 459 Calories; 10.9 g Total Fat (3.6 g Mono, 3.2 g Poly, 3.0 g Sat); 70 mg Cholesterol;
58 g Carbohydrate; 5 g Fibre; 32 g Protein; 1149 mg Sodium*

Paré Pointer
If a traffic light could talk it would say, "Don't look now, I'm changing."

Sole Skillet

This meal's got sole! Lemony, zesty fish
looks mighty fine atop a bed of tasty rice.

Vegetable cocktail (or tomato) juice	2 cups	500 mL
Long grain white rice	1 1/2 cups	375 mL
Diced red pepper	1 1/2 cups	375 mL
Water	1 cup	250 mL
Dried basil	2 tsp.	10 mL
Salt	1/4 tsp.	1 mL
Mayonnaise	1/4 cup	60 mL
Grated lemon zest	2 tsp.	10 mL
Garlic powder	1/8 tsp.	0.5 mL
Pepper	1/8 tsp.	0.5 mL
Sole fillets, any small bones removed, blotted dry	1 lb.	454 g

Combine first 6 ingredients in large frying pan. Bring to a boil. Reduce heat to medium-low. Simmer, covered, for 20 to 30 minutes, without stirring, until rice is tender and liquid is absorbed. Let stand for 5 minutes. Fluff with a fork.

Stir next 4 ingredients in small bowl.

Spread mayonnaise mixture on both sides of fish. Arrange on rice in pan. Broil on centre rack in oven (see Tip, below) for about 5 minutes until fish flakes easily when tested with a fork. Serves 4.

1 serving: 492 Calories; 13.1 g Total Fat (6.6 g Mono, 4.3 g Poly, 1.5 g Sat); 63 mg Cholesterol; 64 g Carbohydrate; 3 g Fibre; 28 g Protein; 641 mg Sodium

 tip When baking or broiling food in a frying pan with a handle that isn't ovenproof, wrap the handle in foil and keep it to the front of the oven, away from the element.

Saucepan Lamb Stew

*Mary had a little lamb, it's true. But what they never told you
was that everywhere that Mary went her saucepan was sure to go, too.
After all, Mary was classically trained at Le Cordon Bleu. And you thought
she was just a sweet little shepherdess! The trick to this treat is using
thyme, rather than spending too much time prepping ingredients.*

Stewing lamb	1 lb.	454 g
All-purpose flour	2 tbsp.	30 mL
Salt	1/2 tsp.	2 mL
Pepper	1/2 tsp.	2 mL
Cooking oil	1 tbsp.	15 mL
Cooking oil	1 tsp.	5 mL
Chopped onion	1 cup	250 mL
Dry (or alcohol-free) red wine	1/4 cup	60 mL
Prepared beef broth	2 1/2 cups	625 mL
Tomato paste (see Tip, page 117)	1 tbsp.	15 mL
Dried thyme	1 tsp.	5 mL
Baby carrots	2 cups	500 mL
Red baby potatoes, halved	1 lb.	454 g
Water	2 tbsp.	30 mL
All-purpose flour	2 tbsp.	30 mL

Put first 4 ingredients into large resealable freezer bag. Seal bag. Toss until coated. Remove lamb. Discard any remaining flour mixture.

Heat first amount of cooking oil in large saucepan on medium. Cook lamb in 2 batches for about 5 minutes per batch, stirring occasionally, until browned. Transfer to large plate. Set aside.

Heat second amount of cooking oil in same saucepan. Add onion. Cook for 5 to 10 minutes, stirring often, until softened.

Add wine. Heat and stir for 1 minute, scraping any brown bits from bottom of saucepan.

Add lamb and next 3 ingredients. Stir. Bring to a boil. Reduce heat to medium-low. Simmer, covered, for 30 minutes.

(continued on next page)

Add carrots and potato. Stir. Bring to a boil. Reduce heat to medium-low. Simmer, covered, for 20 to 30 minutes until lamb and potato are tender.

Stir water into flour in small cup until smooth. Slowly add to lamb mixture, stirring constantly until boiling and thickened. Makes about 6 1/2 cups (1.6 L). Serves 4.

1 serving: 375 Calories; 11.2 g Total Fat (5.3 g Mono, 2.0 g Poly, 2.7 g Sat); 74 mg Cholesterol; 36 g Carbohydrate; 4 g Fibre; 29 g Protein; 899 mg Sodium

Pictured on page 144.

SAUCEPAN BEEF STEW: Use same amount of stewing beef instead of lamb.

 If a recipe calls for less than an entire can of tomato paste, freeze the unopened can for 30 minutes. Open both ends and push the contents through one end. Slice off only what you need. Freeze the remaining paste in a resealable freezer bag or plastic wrap for future use.

Lamb Meatball Skewers

If you haven't tried ground lamb, here's your chance. This easy-to-make entree is a fun initiation for the whole family. Pair with Mediterranean Potatoes, page 45.

Large egg, fork-beaten	1	1
Fine dry bread crumbs	1/4 cup	60 mL
Dried oregano	1/2 tsp.	2 mL
Lemon pepper	1/2 tsp.	2 mL
Seasoned salt	1/2 tsp.	2 mL
Ground nutmeg	1/4 tsp.	1 mL
Ground cinnamon	1/4 tsp.	1 mL
Lean ground lamb	1 lb.	454 g
Medium onion, cut into 24 equal pieces	1	1
Large green pepper, cut into 24 equal pieces	1	1
Large red pepper, cut into 24 equal pieces	1	1
Bamboo skewers (8 inches, 20 cm, each), soaked in water for 10 minutes	8	8
Italian dressing	1/2 cup	125 mL

Combine first 7 ingredients in medium bowl.

Add lamb. Mix well. Divide into 24 equal portions. Roll into balls.

Thread meatballs and next 3 ingredients alternately onto skewers. Place on greased wire rack set in foil-lined baking sheet with sides.

Brush skewers with dressing. Bake in 375°F (190°C) oven for about 30 minutes, turning occasionally and brushing with any remaining dressing, until meatballs are fully cooked, and internal temperature of lamb reaches 160°F (71°C). Serves 4.

1 serving: 580 Calories; 48.7 g Total Fat (22.9 g Mono, 9.2 g Poly, 13.6 g Sat); 149 mg Cholesterol; 14 g Carbohydrate; 2 g Fibre; 22 g Protein; 796 mg Sodium

GRILLED MEATBALL SKEWERS: Preheat gas barbecue to medium. Cook skewers on greased grill for about 15 minutes, turning occasionally and brushing with any remaining dressing, until meatballs are fully cooked, and internal temperature of lamb reaches 160°F (71°C).

Okra And Lamb Casserole

*A favourite of all true belles and beaus, okra makes a tasty
and unexpected contribution to this tomato casserole. Steam
some rice, put it on the table and faster than you can say
"I'll never be hungry again," dinner will be gone with the wind!*

Cooking oil	1 tsp.	5 mL
Lean ground lamb	1 lb.	454 g
Cooking oil	1 tbsp.	15 mL
Fresh (or frozen) okra, cut into 1/2 inch (12 mm) pieces	1 lb.	454 g
Chopped green pepper	1 cup	250 mL
Chopped onion	1/2 cup	125 mL
Can of diced tomatoes (with juice)	14 oz.	398 mL
Granulated sugar	1 tsp.	5 mL
Garlic and herb no-salt seasoning	1 tsp.	5 mL
Dried basil	1/2 tsp.	2 mL
Pepper	1/4 tsp.	1 mL

Heat first amount of cooking oil in large frying pan on medium. Add lamb. Scramble-fry for 5 to 10 minutes until no longer pink. Drain. Transfer to paper towel-lined plate.

Heat second amount of cooking oil in same frying pan. Add okra. Cook for about 5 minutes, stirring occasionally, until starting to brown.

Add green pepper and onion. Cook for about 5 minutes, stirring often, until onion is softened.

Add lamb and remaining 5 ingredients. Stir. Transfer to ungreased 2 quart (2 L) casserole. Bake, covered, in 350°F (175°C) oven for about 45 minutes until boiling. Let stand for about 10 minutes until sauce is slightly thickened. Stir. Makes about 7 cups (1.75 L). Serves 4.

1 serving: 434 Calories; 31.3 g Total Fat (13.6 g Mono, 3.5 g Poly, 11.9 g Sat); 83 mg Cholesterol; 18 g Carbohydrate; 5 g Fibre; 22 g Protein; 348 mg Sodium

Lamb Orzo Stew

Don't know what to make for dinner? Well don't go on the lam just yet.
Go to the lamb, instead, and make this easy, saucy, risotto-like stew.
Serve with buns or garlic bread to sop up the delicious sauce.

Cooking oil	2 tsp.	10 mL
Lamb shanks (see Note)	2 1/2 lbs.	1.1 kg
Chopped onion	2 cups	500 mL
Chopped carrot	1 cup	250 mL
Can of tomato paste	5 1/2 oz.	156 mL
Dry (or alcohol-free) red wine	1 cup	250 mL
Prepared chicken broth	2 cups	500 mL
Water	2 cups	500 mL
Lemon juice	1/4 cup	60 mL
Liquid honey	1 tbsp.	15 mL
Dried rosemary, crushed	1 tsp.	5 mL
Salt	1/4 tsp.	1 mL
Orzo	1 1/2 cups	375 mL
Chopped red pepper	1 cup	250 mL

Heat cooking oil in Dutch oven on medium-high. Add lamb. Cook for 3 to 4 minutes per side until browned.

Add onion and carrot. Cook for about 5 minutes, stirring often, until onion starts to soften.

Add tomato paste. Stir, scraping any brown bits from bottom of pan. Add wine. Heat and stir for 1 minute.

Add next 6 ingredients. Stir. Bring to a boil. Reduce heat to medium-low. Simmer, covered, for about 2 hours until lamb is tender. Transfer lamb to cutting board.

Add orzo and red pepper to broth mixture. Stir. Cook, covered, for 10 to 12 minutes, stirring occasionally, until orzo is tender. Remove shanks to cutting board using slotted spoon. Remove lamb from bones. Discard bones. Chop. Add to orzo mixture. Heat and stir until heated through. Makes about 7 cups (1.75 L). Serves 6.

1 serving: 680 Calories; 28.3 g Total Fat (11.5 g Mono, 2.7 g Poly, 11.5 g Sat); 136 mg Cholesterol; 53 g Carbohydrate; 4 g Fibre; 46 g Protein; 536 mg Sodium

Note: Lamb shanks are commonly found in frozen bulk packages.

Herb-Scented Lamb Kabobs

Making dinner can be quite a job, so get some help from this easy kabob!
The tender lamb infused with fragrant herbs is made to be set atop Cabbage
Noodles, page 62, or served alongside Roasted Veggie Pockets, page 46.

Olive (or cooking) oil	1/3 cup	75 mL
Red wine vinegar	1/4 cup	60 mL
Dried oregano	1 1/2 tsp.	7 mL
Garlic clove, minced (or 1/4 tsp., 1 mL, powder)	1	1
Lemon pepper	1 tsp.	5 mL
Ground coriander	1/2 tsp.	2 mL
Stewing lamb, trimmed of fat	1 lb.	454 g
Bamboo skewers (8 inches, 20 cm, each), soaked in water for 10 minutes	4	4

Combine first 6 ingredients in small bowl. Reserve half of olive oil mixture in small cup for basting sauce.

Put lamb into large resealable freezer bag. Add remaining olive oil mixture. Seal bag. Turn until coated. Let stand in refrigerator for at least 6 hours or overnight, turning occasionally. Drain.

Thread lamb onto skewers. Place on greased broiler pan. Brush kabobs with basting sauce. Broil kabobs on top rack in oven for about 10 minutes, turning once at halftime and brushing with any remaining basting sauce, until desired doneness. Serves 4.

1 serving: 268 Calories; 18.8 g Total Fat (11.9 g Mono, 1.6 g Poly, 3.9 g Sat); 74 mg Cholesterol; trace Carbohydrate; trace Fibre; 23 g Protein; 97 mg Sodium

GRILLED LAMB KABOBS: Preheat gas barbecue to medium. Cook kabobs on greased grill for about 10 minutes, turning once at halftime and brushing with any remaining basting sauce, until desired doneness.

Pictured on page 17.

Couscous And Beans

Couscous goes Greek when it's loaded with olives,
cucumber and feta—it's a tasty twist!

Prepared vegetable (or chicken) broth	1 1/2 cups	375 mL
Plain couscous	1 1/2 cups	375 mL
Can of mixed beans, rinsed and drained	19 oz.	540 mL
Chopped tomato	2 cups	500 mL
Chopped red pepper	1 cup	250 mL
Chopped English cucumber (with peel)	1 cup	250 mL
Chopped kalamata olives	1/4 cup	60 mL
Olive (or cooking) oil	6 tbsp.	100 mL
Balsamic vinegar	3 tbsp.	50 mL
Chopped fresh basil	2 tbsp.	30 mL
Garlic clove, minced (or 1/4 tsp., 1 mL, powder)	1	1
Pepper	1/4 tsp.	1 mL
Crumbled feta cheese	1 cup	250 mL

Measure broth into medium saucepan. Bring to a boil. Add couscous. Stir. Remove from heat. Let stand, covered, for about 5 minutes until couscous is tender and broth is absorbed. Fluff with a fork. Transfer to large bowl. Cool.

Add next 5 ingredients. Toss.

Whisk next 5 ingredients in small bowl until combined. Add to couscous mixture. Toss.

Sprinkle with cheese. Makes 10 cups (2.25 L). Serves 4.

1 serving: 746 Calories; 31.9 g Total Fat (17.9 g Mono, 3.0 g Poly, 9.1 g Sat); 35 mg Cholesterol; 89 g Carbohydrate; 10 g Fibre; 26 g Protein; 1170 mg Sodium

Cottage Broccoli Bake

Tender-crisp broccoli is blanketed with two cheeses and a buttery crumb topping.
Perfect when the mercury's dropping and you're looking for a little warmth.
For our deluxe version of mac 'n' cheese, spoon over hot, buttered macaroni.

Broccoli florets	6 cups	1.5 L
Large eggs	2	2
2% cottage cheese	1 cup	250 mL
Grated sharp (or medium) Cheddar cheese	1 cup	250 mL
Finely chopped green onion	1 tbsp.	15 mL
Lemon pepper	1/2 tsp.	2 mL
Butter (or hard margarine)	2 tbsp.	30 mL
Fine dry bread crumbs	1/3 cup	75 mL
Cornflake crumbs	3 tbsp.	50 mL

Cook broccoli in boiling water in large saucepan until just tender. Drain. Transfer to ungreased 2 quart (2 L) baking dish.

Combine next 5 ingredients in medium bowl. Spoon onto broccoli.

Melt butter in small saucepan. Add bread crumbs and cornflake crumbs. Stir until well mixed. Sprinkle over cottage cheese mixture. Bake, uncovered, in 375°F (190°C) oven for about 30 minutes until golden and set. Serves 6.

1 serving: 218 Calories; 12.7 g Total Fat (2.1 g Mono, 0.6 g Poly, 7.5 g Sat); 92 mg Cholesterol; 12 g Carbohydrate; 2 g Fibre; 14 g Protein; 419 mg Sodium

---

Paré Pointer
A hit and run is only legal in baseball.

Curried Baked Chickpeas

This creative curry combo will keep the compliments coming. This sweet apple, tender chickpea and dark raisin dish is excellent served over steamed rice.

Cans of chickpeas (garbanzo beans), 19 oz. (540 mL), each, rinsed and drained	2	2
Chopped peeled tart apple (such as Granny Smith)	1 cup	250 mL
Chopped onion	3/4 cup	175 mL
Dark raisins	1/2 cup	125 mL
Liquid honey	1/2 cup	125 mL
Sweet pickle relish	1/3 cup	75 mL
Prepared chicken broth	1/4 cup	60 mL
Dijon mustard	1 tbsp.	15 mL
Curry powder	1 tsp.	5 mL

Chopped fresh parsley, for garnish

Combine first 9 ingredients in ungreased 2 quart (2 L) casserole. Bake, covered, in 325°F (160°C) oven for about 45 minutes until apple is tender.

Garnish with parsley. Makes about 5 1/2 cups (1.4 L). Serves 4.

1 serving: 790 Calories; 6.1 g Total Fat (1.6 g Mono, 2.5 g Poly, 0.7 g Sat); 0 mg Cholesterol; 177 g Carbohydrate; 12 g Fibre; 19 g Protein; 2147 mg Sodium

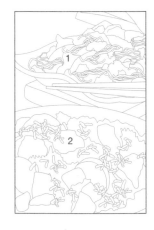

1. Pork Noodle Stri-Fry, page 147
2. Jiffy Jambalaya, page 96

Props courtesy of: Cherison Enterprises Inc.
Stokes

Teriyaki Tofu Pizza

A light, crisp alternative to heavy pizzas. It's a must-try for teriyaki lovers.
Using a ready-made pizza crust makes prep a breeze.

Prebaked pizza crust (12 inch, 30 cm, diameter)	1	1
Thick teriyaki basting sauce	1/3 cup	75 mL
Coarsely grated firm tofu	1 1/3 cups	325 mL
Canned pineapple tidbits, drained	2/3 cup	150 mL
Medium green or red pepper, sliced	1	1
Grated mozzarella cheese	3/4 cup	175 mL
Fresh bean sprouts	1 cup	250 mL
Thinly sliced green onion	2 tbsp.	30 mL

Place pizza crust on greased 12 inch (30 cm) pizza pan. Spread teriyaki sauce on crust, leaving 1/2 inch (12 mm) edge.

Scatter next 3 ingredients over sauce.

Sprinkle with cheese. Bake on centre rack in 475°F (240°C) oven for about 10 minutes until cheese is melted and golden.

Top with bean sprouts and onion. Serves 4.

1 serving: 410 Calories; 10.8 g Total Fat (1.7 g Mono, 1.0 g Poly, 4.0 g Sat); 17 mg Cholesterol, 60 g Carbohydrate; 3 g Fibre; 19 g Protein; 1105 mg Sodium

Pictured at left.

TERIYAKI CHICKEN PIZZA: Use chopped cooked chicken instead of tofu.

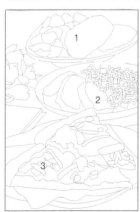

1. Island Chicken Casserole, page 83
2. Ginger Maple Pork, page 148
3. Teriyaki Tofu Pizza, above

Props courtesy of: Cherison Enterprises Inc.
Totally Bamboo

Spicy Vegetable Omelettes

This hot little treat is far too spicy for breakfast fare—this fiery fave deserves
a place at the dinner table! Enough for two but easy to double for four.
Make a complete meal with whole grain toast on the side.

Cooking oil	1 tsp.	5 mL
Sliced fresh white mushrooms	1 cup	250 mL
Chopped green onion	3 tbsp.	50 mL
Chopped tomato	1 cup	250 mL
Chili paste (sambal oelek)	1 tsp.	5 mL
Fresh spinach leaves, lightly packed	1 cup	250 mL
Chopped fresh parsley (or 2 1/4 tsp., 11 mL, flakes)	3 tbsp.	50 mL
Balsamic vinegar	1 tsp.	5 mL
Pepper, sprinkle		
Large eggs	4	4
Milk	2 tbsp.	30 mL
Grated Parmesan cheese	2 tbsp.	30 mL

Heat cooking oil in medium frying pan on medium. Add mushrooms
and green onion. Cook for 5 to 10 minutes, stirring occasionally, until
mushrooms are softened.

Add tomato and chili paste. Heat and stir for about 2 minutes until tomato
is heated through.

Add next 4 ingredients. Heat and stir for about 1 minute until spinach is
just wilted. Remove from heat. Cover to keep warm.

Beat 2 eggs and 1 tbsp. (15 mL) milk in small bowl. Spray small (8 inch,
20 cm) non-stick frying pan with cooking spray. Heat on medium until hot.
Pour egg mixture into pan. Reduce heat to medium-low. When starting to
set at outside edge, tilt pan and gently lift cooked egg mixture with spatula,
easing around pan from outside edge in. Allow uncooked egg mixture to
flow onto bottom of pan until egg is softly set. Slide onto large serving plate.

Drain spinach mixture. Spread half of spinach mixture on half of omelette.
Sprinkle with 1 tbsp. (15 mL) cheese. Fold omelette in half over filling.
Cover to keep warm. Repeat with remaining ingredients. Serves 2.

1 serving: 238 Calories; 14.7 g Total Fat (6.3 g Mono, 2.4 g Poly, 4.6 g Sat); 378 mg Cholesterol;
9 g Carbohydrate; 3 g Fibre; 18 g Protein; 282 mg Sodium

Mushroom Pasta Wedges

This angel hair pasta pizza is a decidedly different
dinner delight. Serve with Sweet Sugar Peas, page 62.

Angel hair pasta	8 oz.	225 g
Large eggs	4	4
2% cottage cheese	1/2 cup	125 mL
Grated Parmesan cheese	1/4 cup	60 mL
Basil pesto	1/4 cup	60 mL
Pepper	1/2 tsp.	2 mL
Olive (or cooking) oil	2 tsp.	10 mL
Sliced fresh white mushrooms	3 cups	750 mL
Green onions, sliced	2	2
Grated Parmesan cheese	1/4 cup	60 mL

Cook pasta in boiling salted water in large uncovered saucepan or Dutch oven for 6 to 8 minutes, stirring occasionally, until tender but firm. Drain. Return to same saucepan.

Process next 5 ingredients in blender or food processor until smooth. Add to pasta. Toss.

Heat olive oil in medium frying pan on medium-high. Add mushrooms. Cook for about 10 minutes, stirring occasionally, until softened and liquid is evaporated. Add to pasta mixture.

Add green onion. Toss. Spread pasta mixture in greased foil-lined 12 inch (30 cm) pizza pan. Press pasta mixture firmly with back of spoon.

Sprinkle with second amount of Parmesan cheese. Bake in 375°F (190°C) oven for 35 to 40 minutes until edge is golden. Let stand for 10 minutes. Serves 6.

1 serving: 319 Calories; 13.6 g Total Fat (3.4 g Mono, 0.8 g Poly, 3.9 g Sat); 135 mg Cholesterol; 30 g Carbohydrate; 1 g Fibre; 17 g Protein; 363 mg Sodium

Barley-Stuffed Peppers

Your vegetarian friends will weep for joy when they see these
wholesome stuffed peppers filled with barley, mushrooms and
havarti cheese. This is how you do vegetarian right!

Cooking (or olive) oil	1 tbsp.	15 mL
Chopped fresh white mushrooms	2 cups	500 mL
Pearl barley	1 cup	250 mL
Garlic cloves, minced (or 1/2 tsp., 2 mL, powder)	2	2
Prepared vegetable (or chicken) broth	2 1/2 cups	625 mL
Package of veggie ground round (see Note)	12 oz.	340 g
Vegetable cocktail juice	1 cup	250 mL
Italian seasoning	1 tsp.	5 mL
Sliced green onion	1/4 cup	60 mL
Large red peppers, halved lengthwise	4	4
Grated havarti cheese	1 1/2 cups	375 mL

Heat cooking oil in large frying pan on medium-high. Add next 3 ingredients. Cook for about 5 minutes, stirring occasionally, until barley is toasted and mushrooms are softened.

Add next 4 ingredients. Stir. Bring to a boil. Reduce heat to medium. Boil gently, uncovered, for about 30 minutes, stirring occasionally, until barley is almost tender. Remove from heat.

Add green onion. Stir.

Arrange red pepper halves in greased 9 x 13 inch (22 x 33 cm) baking dish. Fill with barley mixture.

Sprinkle with cheese. Bake in 400°F (205°C) oven for 15 to 20 minutes until red pepper is tender-crisp and cheese is melted. Serves 4.

1 serving: 573 Calories; 20.8 g Total Fat (2.5 g Mono, 1.8 g Poly, 11.3 g Sat); 38 mg Cholesterol; 61 g Carbohydrate; 17 g Fibre; 34 g Protein; 1319 mg Sodium

Note: Veggie ground round is available in the produce section of your grocery store.

Potato Egg Muffins

A muffin for a dinner entree? You bet! Full of potatoes and cheese, this savoury delight is made to please. Outstanding with a green salad for a nice, light meal.

Chive and onion cream cheese	3 tbsp.	50 mL
Milk	3 tbsp.	50 mL
Large eggs	4	4
Frozen shredded hash brown potatoes	4 cups	1 L
Grated mozzarella cheese	3/4 cup	175 mL
Sliced green onion	1/4 cup	60 mL
Salt	1/2 tsp.	2 mL
Pepper	1/4 tsp.	1 mL

Mash cream cheese and milk with fork in small bowl.

Beat eggs in medium bowl until frothy. Add cream cheese mixture. Stir.

Add remaining 5 ingredients. Stir. Spoon into 8 greased muffin cups. Bake in 350°F (175°C) oven for 30 to 35 minutes until golden and set. Let stand in pan on wire rack for 5 minutes. Run knife around edges of muffin cups to loosen. Serves 4.

1 serving: 356 Calories; 14.9 g Total Fat (3.7 g Mono, 1.5 g Poly, 7.5 g Sat); 215 mg Cholesterol; 40 g Carbohydrate; 4 g Fibre; 16 g Protein; 541 mg Sodium

SMOKED SALMON EGG MUFFINS: Use smoked salmon cream cheese instead of chive and onion.

VEGETABLE ASIAGO EGG MUFFINS: Use vegetable cream cheese instead of chive and onion, and grated Asiago cheese instead of mozzarella.

ROASTED PEPPER EGG MUFFINS: Use roasted red pepper cream cheese instead of chive and onion, and grated Swiss cheese instead of mozzarella.

Greek Couscous Pizza

The toppings are all Greek to us, but the crust is a crunchy combination of walnuts and couscous—you may never go back to plain old pizza dough again.

CRUST

Prepared vegetable broth	3/4 cup	175 mL
Plain couscous	3/4 cup	175 mL
Finely chopped walnuts	1 cup	250 mL
Grated mozzarella cheese	1/2 cup	125 mL
Large egg, fork-beaten	1	1

TOPPING

Cooking oil	1 tsp.	5 mL
Sliced fresh white mushrooms	1 1/2 cups	375 mL
Can of diced tomatoes, drained	14 oz.	398 mL
Thinly sliced zucchini (with peel)	1 1/2 cups	375 mL
Italian seasoning	1/2 tsp.	2 mL
Grated mozzarella cheese	1 cup	250 mL
Crumbled feta cheese	1/2 cup	125 mL

Crust: Measure broth into small saucepan. Bring to a boil. Add couscous. Stir. Remove from heat. Let stand, covered, for about 5 minutes until couscous is tender and broth is absorbed. Fluff with a fork.

Add next 3 ingredients. Stir. Press into bottom and up side of greased 12 inch (30 cm) pizza pan. Bake in 400°F (205°C) oven for about 10 minutes until set and golden.

Topping: Heat cooking oil in large frying pan on medium-high. Add mushrooms. Cook for about 5 minutes, stirring occasionally, until softened and liquid is evaporated. Reduce heat to medium.

Add next 3 ingredients. Cook for about 5 minutes, stirring occasionally, until zucchini is tender. Spread on couscous crust.

Sprinkle with mozzarella and feta cheese. Bake in 400°F (205°C) oven for about 15 minutes until cheese is melted and golden. Serves 6.

1 serving: 377 Calories; 24.1 g Total Fat (5.1 g Mono, 10.2 g Poly, 7.4 g Sat); 66 mg Cholesterol; 27 g Carbohydrate; 3 g Fibre; 16 g Protein; 513 mg Sodium

Potato Tofu Frittata

Whether it's brunch, lunch or dinner, a frittata fits the bill.
Flavoured with basil, tomato and leek, this meatless dish doesn't
skimp on taste. Serve with the green salad of your choice.

Red baby potatoes, quartered	6 oz.	170 g
Cooking oil	1 tbsp.	15 mL
Sliced leek (white part only)	1 1/2 cups	375 mL
Coarsely grated firm tofu	1 1/3 cups	325 mL
Green onions, sliced	2	2
Large eggs	6	6
Chopped fresh basil	1/4 cup	60 mL
Salt, sprinkle		
Pepper, sprinkle		
Roma (plum) tomatoes, sliced	2	2
Chopped fresh basil, for garnish		

Cook potato in boiling salted water in small saucepan until tender. Drain.

Heat cooking oil in large frying pan on medium. Add leek. Cook for about 5 minutes, stirring often, until tender.

Add potato, tofu and onion. Cook for about 3 minutes, stirring occasionally, until onion is softened.

Beat eggs in medium bowl until frothy. Add next 3 ingredients. Stir. Pour over potato mixture. Do not stir. Reduce heat to medium-low. Cook, covered, for about 5 minutes until bottom is golden and top is almost set. Remove from heat.

Arrange tomato on top. Broil on centre rack in oven for 3 to 4 minutes until frittata is set (see Tip, page 115).

Garnish with basil. Serves 4.

1 serving: 229 Calories; 12.3 g Total Fat (5.5 g Mono, 2.9 g Poly, 2.8 g Sat); 279 mg Cholesterol; 16 g Carbohydrate; 2 g Fibre; 14 g Protein; 120 mg Sodium

Pork Marsala

An elegant wine-simmered dish that's remarkably easy to prepare.
Serve over buttered egg noodles or creamy mashed potatoes
with Walnut Green Salad, page 12, on the side.

All-purpose flour	1/4 cup	60 mL
Salt	1/4 tsp.	1 mL
Pepper	1/8 tsp.	0.5 mL
Pork tenderloin, trimmed of fat and cut diagonally into 1/4 inch (6 mm) slices	1 lb.	454 g
Olive (or cooking) oil	1 tbsp.	15 mL
Butter (or hard margarine)	1 tbsp.	15 mL
Sliced fresh white mushrooms	2 cups	500 mL
Prepared chicken broth	1 cup	250 mL
Marsala wine	1/4 cup	60 mL

Chopped fresh parsley, for garnish

Combine first 3 ingredients in small shallow dish.

Press both sides of pork in flour mixture. Transfer pork to large plate. Set remaining flour mixture aside.

Heat olive oil and butter in large frying pan on medium-high. Add pork. Cook for about 1 minute per side until browned. Transfer to separate large plate. Reduce heat to medium.

Cook mushrooms in same frying pan for about 5 minutes, stirring occasionally, until softened and liquid is evaporated. Sprinkle with remaining flour mixture. Heat and stir for 1 minute.

Slowly add broth and wine, stirring constantly and scraping any brown bits from bottom of pan. Heat and stir for about 5 minutes until boiling and thickened. Add pork. Reduce heat to medium-low. Simmer, covered, for about 10 minutes, stirring occasionally, until desired doneness. Remove to large serving bowl.

Garnish with parsley. Makes about 6 cups (1.5 L). Serves 4.

1 serving: 266 Calories; 9.6 g Total Fat (4.7 g Mono, 0.9 g Poly, 3.4 g Sat); 74 mg Cholesterol; 9 g Carbohydrate; 1 g Fibre; 30 g Protein; 420 mg Sodium

Pictured on front cover.

Pineapple Pork Kabobs

The islands await. Coconut, pineapple and pork—sounds like a luau to us! Serve with Sweet Potato Salad, page 11.

Can of coconut milk	14 oz.	398 mL
Sweet chili sauce	2 tbsp.	30 mL
Brown sugar, packed	1 tbsp.	15 mL
Grated lime zest	1 tsp.	5 mL
Fish (or soy) sauce	1 tsp.	5 mL
Finely grated gingerroot (or 1/4 tsp., 1 mL, ground ginger)	1 tsp.	5 mL
Pork tenderloin, trimmed of fat and cubed	1 lb.	454 g
Cubed fresh pineapple (or 14 oz., 398 mL, can of pineapple chunks, drained)	3 cups	750 mL
Bamboo skewers (8 inches, 20 cm, each), soaked in water for 10 minutes	8	8

Combine first 6 ingredients in large bowl.

Add pork. Stir. Let stand, covered, in refrigerator for 3 to 5 hours. Drain coconut milk mixture into small saucepan. Bring to a boil on medium. Boil gently, uncovered, for at least 5 minutes, stirring occasionally, until slightly thickened.

Thread pork and pineapple alternately onto skewers. Place on greased broiler pan. Broil on centre rack in oven for 20 to 25 minutes, turning occasionally and brushing with coconut milk mixture, until desired doneness. Serves 4.

1 serving: 409 Calories; 24.2 g Total Fat (2.2 g Mono, 0.6 g Poly, 19.8 g Sat); 67 mg Cholesterol; 21 g Carbohydrate; 2 g Fibre; 30 g Protein; 188 mg Sodium

GRILLED PINEAPPLE PORK KABOBS: Preheat gas barbecue to medium. Cook kabobs on greased grill for about 15 minutes, turning occasionally and brushing with coconut milk mixture, until desired doneness.

Island Pork Fajitas

Mango, lime and jalapeño pepper give these fajitas
a tasty Caribbean flair, while jicama adds a great crunchy texture.
The pork may be marinated overnight in the refrigerator.

Diced red onion	1/2 cup	125 mL
Fresh jalapeño peppers, finely diced (see Tip, page 46)	2	2
Garlic cloves, minced (or 3/4 tsp., 4 mL, powder)	3	3
Chili powder	2 tsp.	10 mL
Chopped fresh (or frozen) mango	1 1/4 cups	300 mL
Diced peeled jicama	1 cup	250 mL
Chopped fresh cilantro or parsley	2 tbsp.	30 mL
Lime juice	2 tbsp.	30 mL
Lime juice	3 tbsp.	50 mL
Boneless centre-cut pork chops	1 lb.	454 g
Flour tortillas (9 inch, 22 cm, diameter), see Note	8	8
Fresh spinach leaves, lightly packed	2 cups	500 mL

Combine first 4 ingredients in medium bowl. Transfer half of onion mixture to large resealable freezer bag.

Add next 4 ingredients to remaining onion mixture in bowl. Stir. Chill.

Add second amount of lime juice to onion mixture in freezer bag. Shake gently until combined.

Add pork. Seal bag. Turn until coated. Let stand in refrigerator for at least 2 hours. Arrange pork on greased broiler pan. Broil on top rack in oven for about 5 minutes per side until desired doneness. Remove to cutting board. Let stand for 5 minutes. Cut into thin slices.

Arrange pork down centre of tortillas.

Top with mango mixture and spinach. Fold bottom ends of tortillas over filling. Fold in sides, slightly overlapping, leaving top ends open. Serves 4.

1 serving: 680 Calories; 24.4 g Total Fat (11.2 g Mono, 3.7 g Poly, 7.4 g Sat); 76 mg Cholesterol; 80 g Carbohydrate; 8 g Fibre; 35 g Protein; 878 mg Sodium

(continued on next page)

Note: Tortillas may be wrapped in foil and heated in the oven if desired.

GRILLED PORK FAJITAS: Preheat gas barbecue to medium. Cook pork on greased grill for 3 to 5 minutes per side until desired doneness. Remove to cutting board. Let stand for 5 minutes. Cut into thin slices.

Pork In Plum Sauce

Plum delicious! This easy-to-make dish is
delectable with Baked Fragrant Rice, page 61.

Water	1/3 cup	75 mL
Soy sauce	2 tbsp.	30 mL
Hoisin sauce	2 tbsp.	30 mL
Cornstarch	1 tbsp.	15 mL
Dry sherry	1 tbsp.	15 mL
Sesame oil	2 tsp.	10 mL
Pork tenderloin, trimmed of fat, halved, lengthwise, cut into 1/4 inch (6 mm) slices	1 1/2 lbs.	680 g
Plum sauce	1 cup	250 mL
Chili paste (sambal oelek)	1 tsp.	5 mL
Pepper	1/4 tsp.	1 mL
Cooking oil	1 tbsp.	15 mL
Green onion, thinly sliced	1	1

Combine first 6 ingredients in large bowl.

Add pork. Stir until coated. Let stand, covered, in refrigerator for 1 hour. Drain, reserving soy sauce mixture in medium saucepan.

Add next 3 ingredients to soy sauce mixture. Stir. Bring to a boil. Reduce heat to medium. Boil gently for at least 5 minutes until slightly thickened.

Heat wok or large frying pan on medium-high until very hot. Add cooking oil. Add pork. Stir-fry for 3 minutes. Add plum sauce mixture. Cook for 1 to 2 minutes until desired doneness. Remove to large serving bowl.

Sprinkle with green onion. Makes about 4 cups (1 L). Serves 6.

1 serving: 290 Calories; 7.3 g Total Fat (3.4 g Mono, 2.0 g Poly, 1.5 g Sat); 67 mg Cholesterol; 26 g Carbohydrate; 1 g Fibre; 28 g Protein; 850 mg Sodium

Pork Pot Roast

Call it the roast with the most. The flavours of Dijon and pickling spice add a tangy twist to the traditional pot roast. Serve with pickled beets on the side.

Cooking oil	1 tsp.	5 mL
Boneless pork shoulder butt roast	3 lbs.	1.4 kg
Medium onions, quartered	3	3
Apple juice	1 cup	250 mL
Dijon mustard	1 tbsp.	15 mL
Mixed pickling spice	1 tbsp.	15 mL
Cubed yellow turnip	3 cups	750 mL
Salt	1/2 tsp.	2 mL
Frozen Brussels sprouts, thawed	3 cups	750 mL
Large peeled yams (or sweet potatoes), quartered lengthwise and cut into 2 inch (5 cm) pieces	3	3
Water	1/4 cup	60 mL
All-purpose flour	1 1/2 tbsp.	25 mL

Heat cooking oil in large frying pan on medium-high. Add roast. Cook for about 5 minutes, turning occasionally, until browned on all sides. Transfer to large roasting pan. Set aside. Reduce heat to medium.

Cook onion in same frying pan for about 5 minutes, stirring often, until browned.

Add next 3 ingredients. Heat and stir for 1 minute, scraping any brown bits from bottom of pan. Poke holes in roast with a meat fork. Pour apple juice mixture over top.

Arrange turnip around roast in pan. Sprinkle with salt. Cook, covered, in 350°F (175°C) oven for 1 hour.

Add Brussels sprouts and yam. Cook, covered, for another 40 to 50 minutes until vegetables are tender and meat thermometer inserted into thickest part of roast reads at least 155°F (68°C) or desired doneness. Remove roast to cutting board. Cover with foil. Let stand for 10 minutes. Remove vegetables to large serving bowl. Cover to keep warm. Strain drippings through sieve into small saucepan. Skim any fat from surface. Bring to a boil on medium.

(continued on next page)

Stir water into flour in small cup until smooth. Slowly add to drippings, stirring constantly until boiling and thickened. Slice roast. Makes 12 servings (2 to 3 oz., 57 to 85 g each, cooked weight). Serve with vegetables and gravy. Serves 12.

1 serving: 305 Calories; 15.1 g Total Fat (6.5 g Mono, 1.6 g Poly, 5.4 g Sat); 51 mg Cholesterol; 24 g Carbohydrate; 3 g Fibre; 19 g Protein; 200 mg Sodium

Pictured on page 71.

Cajun Cutlets

The kindest cut(let) of all! Top with a squeeze of lemon and serve with Potato And Green Bean Salad, page 21. Or sandwich in ciabatta buns, top with your favourite condiments and serve coleslaw on the side.

All-purpose flour	1/3 cup	75 mL
Cajun seasoning	1 tsp.	5 mL
Salt	1/2 tsp.	2 mL
Pepper	1/4 tsp.	1 mL
Large egg	1	1
Milk	3 tbsp.	50 mL
Fine dry bread crumbs	3/4 cup	175 mL
Grated Parmesan cheese	2 tbsp.	30 ml
Pork cutlets (about 4 oz., 113 g, each)	4	4
Cooking oil	2 tbsp.	30 mL
Lemon wedges, for garnish		

Combine first 4 ingredients in small shallow dish.

Beat egg and milk in small bowl.

Stir bread crumbs and cheese in separate small shallow dish.

Press both sides of pork in flour mixture. Dip into egg mixture. Press in crumb mixture until coated. Heat cooking oil in large frying pan on medium. Add pork. Cook for about 3 minutes per side until desired doneness and crumb coating is golden. Remove to large serving plate.

Garnish with lemon wedges. Serves 4.

1 serving: 488 Calories; 31.0 g Total Fat (14.6 g Mono, 4.7 g Poly, 9.0 g Sat); 117 mg Cholesterol; 23 g Carbohydrate; 1 g Fibre; 27 g Protein; 750 mg Sodium

Pictured on page 143.

Ribbon Zucchini Frittata

A smoky ham and cheese frittata that's all dressed up in ribbons
of green. Superbly satisfying with Spiced Yam Hash, page 55.

Olive (or cooking) oil	1 1/2 tbsp.	25 mL
Large zucchini (with peel), cut lengthwise into 1/4 inch (6 mm) slices	1	1
Large eggs	8	8
Julienned deli ham (see Tip, below)	1 cup	250 mL
Grated sharp Cheddar cheese	1/2 cup	125 mL
Chopped fresh parsley	3 tbsp.	50 mL
Milk	1 tbsp.	15 mL
Salt	1/8 tsp.	0.5 mL
Pepper	1/4 tsp.	1 mL
Olive (or cooking) oil	1 1/2 tsp.	7 mL
Grated sharp Cheddar cheese	1/2 cup	125 mL
Ground nutmeg	1/4 tsp.	1 mL

Heat first amount of olive oil in large frying pan on medium-high. Add and cook zucchini in several batches for 2 to 3 minutes per side until browned. Transfer to large plate. Set aside.

Beat eggs in large bowl until frothy.

Add next 6 ingredients. Stir.

Heat second amount of olive oil in same frying pan on medium. Add egg mixture. Reduce heat to medium-low. Cook, covered, for about 10 minutes until bottom is golden and top is almost set. Remove from heat.

Arrange zucchini on top. Sprinkle with second amount of cheese and nutmeg. Broil on centre rack in oven for 2 to 3 minutes until cheese is melted and golden (see Tip, page 115). Serves 4.

1 serving: 363 Calories; 26.3 g Total Fat (9.3 g Mono, 2.1 g Poly, 10.1 g Sat); 413 mg Cholesterol; 6 g Carbohydrate; 1 g Fibre; 26 g Protein; 853 mg Sodium

Pictured on page 54.

 tip   To julienne, cut into very thin strips that resemble matchsticks.

Satay Pork Skewers

Serve these coconut, lime and chili-marinated skewers to your dinner guests and they just might satay all night! A veritable feast with Lemon-Kissed Couscous, page 60.

Prepared chicken broth	1/2 cup	125 mL
Smooth peanut butter	1/4 cup	60 mL
Sweet chili sauce	2 tbsp.	30 mL
Coconut milk powder	2 tbsp.	30 mL
Lime juice	4 tsp.	20 mL
Mirin (see Note), or rice vinegar	1 tbsp.	15 mL
Hoisin sauce	1 tbsp.	15 mL
Finely grated gingerroot (or 1/4 tsp., 1 mL, ground ginger)	1 1/2 tsp.	7 mL
Pepper	1/4 tsp.	1 mL
Pork tenderloin, trimmed of fat, halved lengthwise, cut diagonally into 1/4 inch (6 mm) slices	1 lb.	454 g
Bamboo skewers (8 inches, 20 cm, each), soaked in water for 10 minutes	16	16

Process first 9 ingredients in blender or food processor until smooth. Reserve half of broth mixture in small bowl for dipping sauce. Chill.

Put pork into large resealable freezer bag. Add remaining broth mixture. Seal bag. Turn until coated. Let stand in refrigerator for at least 3 hours, turning occasionally. Drain.

Thread pork, accordion-style, onto skewers. Place skewers on greased broiler pan. Broil on top rack in oven for about 2 minutes per side until desired doneness. Serve with warmed dipping sauce. Serves 4.

1 serving: 252 Calories; 10.8 g Total Fat (4.3 g Mono, 2.1 g Poly, 3.8 g Sat); 67 mg Cholesterol; 6 g Carbohydrate; 1 g Fibre; 31 g Protein; 186 mg Sodium

Note: Mirin is a Japanese sweet cooking rice wine. It is available in specialty Asian grocery stores.

GRILLED PORK SKEWERS: Preheat gas barbecue to medium-high. Cook skewers on greased grill for about 2 minutes per side until desired doneness and grill marks appear. Serve with warmed dipping sauce.

Sausage Pepper Skillet

Peppers abound in this colourful skillet. First-rate with Asiago Polenta, page 40.

Olive (or cooking) oil	2 tsp.	10 mL
Hot Italian sausages, cut into 1 inch (2.5 cm) pieces	1 lb.	454 g
Sliced green pepper	1 1/2 cups	375 mL
Sliced red pepper	1 1/2 cups	375 mL
Sliced orange pepper	1 1/2 cups	375 mL
Sliced red onion	3/4 cup	175 mL
Prepared chicken broth	1/2 cup	125 mL
Balsamic vinegar	3 tbsp.	50 mL
Sun-dried tomatoes, softened in boiling water for 10 minutes before chopping	2 tbsp.	30 mL

Heat olive oil in large frying pan on medium. Add sausage. Cook for 6 to 8 minutes, stirring often, until browned. Transfer with slotted spoon to paper towels to drain.

Heat 2 tsp. (10 mL) drippings in same frying pan. Add next 4 ingredients. Stir. Cook, covered, for 5 to 10 minutes, stirring occasionally, until onion is softened and peppers are tender-crisp.

Add sausage and remaining 3 ingredients. Heat and stir for about 5 minutes, scraping any brown bits from bottom of pan, until heated through. Makes about 6 cups (1.5 L). Serves 4.

1 serving: 460 Calories; 32.7 g Total Fat (15.6 g Mono, 4.3 g Poly, 11.0 g Sat); 90 mg Cholesterol; 16 g Carbohydrate; 3 g Fibre; 26 g Protein; 1190 mg Sodium

Pictured at right.

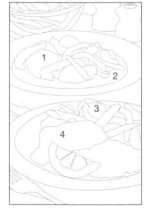

1. Sausage Pepper Skillet, above
2. Asiago Polenta, page 40
3. Potato And Green Bean Salad, page 21
4. Cajun Cutlets, page 139

Ground Pork Patties

*Delicious, thick, juicy patties with a boisterous barbecue flavour—
the secret's in the oyster sauce. Grated Carrot Salad, page 10, and
French fries or mashed potatoes will make dinner complete.*

Large egg, fork-beaten	1	1
Fine dry bread crumbs	1/3 cup	75 mL
Finely chopped onion	1/4 cup	60 mL
Barbecue sauce	3 tbsp.	50 mL
Ketchup	3 tbsp.	50 mL
Oyster sauce	1 tbsp.	15 mL
Garlic cloves, minced (or 1/2 tsp., 2 mL, powder)	2	2
Salt	1/2 tsp.	2 mL
Pepper	1/4 tsp.	1 mL
Lean ground pork	1 lb.	454 g

Combine first 9 ingredients in large bowl.

Add pork. Mix well. Divide into 12 equal portions. Shape into 3 inch (7.5 cm) diameter patties. Arrange on greased broiler pan. Broil on centre rack in oven for 6 to 8 minutes per side until no longer pink inside. Serves 4.

1 serving: 220 Calories; 8.0 g Total Fat (0.8 g Mono, 0.4 g Poly, 3.0 g Sat); 112 mg Cholesterol; 13 g Carbohydrate, 1 g Fibre, 25 g Protein, 733 mg Sodium

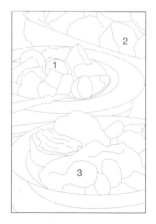

1. Saucepan Lamb Stew, page 116
2. Roasted Garlic Pesto Muffins, page 38
3. Chorizo Sausage Gnocchi, page 146

Props courtesy of: Danesco Inc.
                             Out of the Fire Studio

Chorizo Sausage Gnocchi

Gnocchi, gnocchi. Who's there? Company called—and now that they're here—
with this hearty pasta dish on the table, there'll be lots of good cheer!

Cooking oil	1/2 tsp.	2 mL
Chorizo sausages, cut into 1/4 inch (6 mm) slices	2	2
Cooking oil	1 tbsp.	15 mL
Chopped eggplant (with peel)	2 cups	500 mL
Sliced fresh white mushrooms	1 cup	250 mL
Chopped onion	1 cup	250 mL
Garlic cloves, minced (or 1/2 tsp., 2 mL, powder)	2	2
Tomato pasta sauce	2 cups	500 mL
Chopped fresh parsley (or 1 tbsp., 15 mL, flakes)	1/4 cup	60 mL
Salt	1/4 tsp.	1 mL
Pepper	1/4 tsp.	1 mL
Package of fresh gnocchi	16 1/2 oz.	500 g

Grated Cheddar cheese, for garnish

Heat first amount of cooking oil in large frying pan on medium-high. Add sausage. Cook for about 5 minutes, stirring occasionally, until browned. Transfer with slotted spoon to paper towels to drain. Discard drippings.

Heat second amount of cooking oil in same pan on medium. Add next 4 ingredients. Cook for 5 to 10 minutes, stirring often, until onion is softened.

Add sausage and next 4 ingredients. Heat and stir for about 2 minutes until heated through.

Cook gnocchi in boiling salted water in large uncovered saucepan for about 1 minute until just tender. Transfer with slotted spoon to sausage mixture. Stir gently.

Garnish individual servings with cheese. Makes about 6 1/2 cups (1.6 L). Serves 4.

1 serving: 405 Calories; 23.7 g Total Fat (7.6 g Mono, 1.9 g Poly, 9.6 g Sat); 38 mg Cholesterol; 40 g Carbohydrate; 6 g Fibre; 10 g Protein; 1038 mg Sodium

Pictured on page 144.

Pork Noodle Stir-Fry

Use your noodles and spend as little time making dinner as possible! Try it with your favourite vegetables or save time with a precut veggie blend from your grocery store.

Fresh, thin Chinese-style egg noodles, cut in half	8 oz.	225 g
Sesame (or cooking) oil	1 tbsp.	15 mL
Boneless pork loin chops, trimmed of fat and cut crosswise into thin strips	1 lb.	454 g
Sesame (or cooking) oil	2 tsp.	10 mL
Fresh mixed stir-fry vegetables	5 cups	1.25 L
Prepared chicken broth	1/2 cup	125 mL
Garlic cloves, minced (or 1/2 tsp., 2 mL, powder)	2	2
Finely grated gingerroot (or 1/2 tsp., 2 mL, ground ginger)	2 tsp.	10 mL
Sweet chili sauce	1/4 cup	60 mL
Hoisin sauce	1/4 cup	60 mL

Cook noodles in boiling salted water in large uncovered saucepan or Dutch oven for about 3 minutes, stirring occasionally, until tender but firm. Drain, reserving 1 cup (250 mL) cooking water.

Heat wok or large frying pan on medium-high until very hot. Add first amount of sesame oil. Add pork. Stir-fry for about 5 minutes until browned. Transfer to large plate. Set aside.

Add second amount of sesame oil to hot wok. Add next 4 ingredients. Stir-fry for about 3 minutes until vegetables start to soften.

Add reserved cooking water, chili sauce and hoisin sauce. Stir. Add noodles and pork. Toss. Cook, covered, for about 2 minutes until vegetables are tender-crisp and noodles are heated through. Makes about 8 cups (2 L). Serves 4.

1 serving: 416 Calories; 11.9 g Total Fat (4.5 g Mono, 3.1 g Poly, 2.7 g Sat); 81 mg Cholesterol; 43 g Carbohydrate; 3 g Fibre; 33 g Protein; 564 mg Sodium

Pictured on page 125.

Ginger Maple Pork

Pork tenderloin is paired with a packet of flavourful rice. Garnish the rice with sliced green onion, and complete with a salad on the side.

Maple (or maple-flavoured) syrup	1/3 cup	75 mL
Finely grated gingerroot (or 3/4 tsp., 4 mL, ground ginger)	1 tbsp.	15 mL
Garlic clove, minced (or 1/4 tsp., 1 mL, powder)	1	1
Pork tenderloin, trimmed of fat	1 lb.	454 g
Salt	1/4 tsp.	1 mL
Pepper	1/8 tsp.	0.5 mL
Cooked long grain white rice (about 2/3 cup, 150 mL, uncooked)	2 cups	500 mL
Chopped fresh spinach, lightly packed	1/2 cup	125 mL
Thinly sliced green onion	2 tbsp.	30 mL
Sliced natural almonds, toasted (see Tip, page 20)	2 tbsp.	30 mL
Rice vinegar	2 tsp.	10 mL
Finely grated gingerroot (or 1/8 tsp., 0.5 mL, ground ginger)	1/2 tsp.	2 mL
Salt	1/4 tsp.	1 mL
Sesame oil (optional)	1/2 tsp.	2 mL

Combine first 3 ingredients in small bowl. Set aside.

Sprinkle tenderloin with first amount of salt and pepper. Preheat gas barbecue to medium. Cook tenderloin on greased grill for 15 minutes, turning occasionally. Brush with syrup mixture. Cook for another 15 to 20 minutes until meat thermometer inserted into thickest part of tenderloin reads at least 155°F (68°C) or desired doneness. Remove to cutting board. Cover with foil. Let stand for 10 minutes.

Combine remaining 8 ingredients in medium bowl. Transfer to greased sheet of heavy-duty (or double layer of regular) foil. Fold edges of foil together over rice mixture to enclose. Fold ends to seal completely. Place packet, seam-side up, on ungreased grill. Cook for about 15 minutes until heated through. Cut tenderloin into 12 slices. Serve with rice. Serves 4.

1 serving: 337 Calories; 5.2 g Total Fat (2.5 g Mono, 1.0 g Poly, 1.3 g Sat); 67 mg Cholesterol; 41 g Carbohydrate; 1 g Fibre; 30 g Protein; 356 mg Sodium

Pictured on page 126.

Measurement Tables

Throughout this book measurements are given in Conventional and Metric measure. To compensate for differences between the two measurements due to rounding, a full metric measure is not always used. The cup used is the standard 8 fluid ounce. Temperature is given in degrees Fahrenheit and Celsius. Baking pan measurements are in inches and centimetres as well as quarts and litres. An exact metric conversion is given below as well as the working equivalent (Metric Standard Measure).

Spoons

Conventional Measure	Metric Exact Conversion Millilitre (mL)	Metric Standard Measure Millilitre (mL)
1/8 teaspoon (tsp.)	0.6 mL	0.5 mL
1/4 teaspoon (tsp.)	1.2 mL	1 mL
1/2 teaspoon (tsp.)	2.4 mL	2 mL
1 teaspoon (tsp.)	4.7 mL	5 mL
2 teaspoons (tsp.)	9.4 mL	10 mL
1 tablespoon (tbsp.)	14.2 mL	15 mL

Cups

Conventional Measure	Metric Exact Conversion Millilitre (mL)	Metric Standard Measure Millilitre (mL)
1/4 cup (4 tbsp.)	56.8 mL	60 mL
1/3 cup (5 1/3 tbsp.)	75.6 mL	75 mL
1/2 cup (8 tbsp.)	113.7 mL	125 mL
2/3 cup (10 2/3 tbsp.)	151.2 mL	150 mL
3/4 cup (12 tbsp.)	170.5 mL	175 mL
1 cup (16 tbsp.)	227.3 mL	250 ml
4 1/2 cups	1022.9 mL	1000 mL (1 L)

Oven Temperatures

Fahrenheit (°F)	Celsius (°C)
175°	80°
200°	95°
225°	110°
250°	120°
275°	140°
300°	150°
325°	160°
350°	175°
375°	190°
400°	205°
425°	220°
450°	230°
475°	240°
500°	260°

Dry Measurements

Conventional Measure Ounces (oz.)	Metric Exact Conversion Grams (g)	Metric Standard Measure Grams (g)
1 oz.	28.3 g	28 g
2 oz.	56.7 g	57 g
3 oz.	85.0 g	85 g
4 oz.	113.4 g	125 g
5 oz.	141.7 g	140 g
6 oz.	170.1 g	170 g
7 oz.	198.4 g	200 g
8 oz.	226.8 g	250 g
16 oz.	453.6 g	500 g
32 oz.	907.2 g	1000 g (1 kg)

Pans

Conventional Inches	Metric Centimetres
8x8 inch	20x20 cm
9x9 inch	22x22 cm
9x13 inch	22x33 cm
10x15 inch	25x38 cm
11x17 inch	28x43 cm
8x2 inch round	20x5 cm
9x2 inch round	22x5 cm
10x4 1/2 inch tube	25x11 cm
8x4x3 inch loaf	20x10x7.5 cm
9x5x3 inch loaf	22x12.5x7.5 cm

Casseroles

CANADA & BRITAIN		UNITED STATES	
Standard Size Casserole	Exact Metric Measure	Standard Size Casserole	Exact Metric Measure
1 qt. (5 cups)	1.13 L	1 qt. (4 cups)	900 mL
1 1/2 qts. (7 1/2 cups)	1.69 L	1 1/2 qts. (6 cups)	1.35 L
2 qts. (10 cups)	2.25 L	2 qts. (8 cups)	1.8 L
2 1/2 qts. (12 1/2 cups)	2.81 L	2 1/2 qts. (10 cups)	2.25 L
3 qts. (15 cups)	3.38 L	3 qts. (12 cups)	2.7 L
4 qts. (20 cups)	4.5 L	4 qts. (16 cups)	3.6 L
5 qts. (25 cups)	5.63 L	5 qts. (20 cups)	4.5 L

Recipe Index

A

B

150

C

151

L

M

N

O

153

S

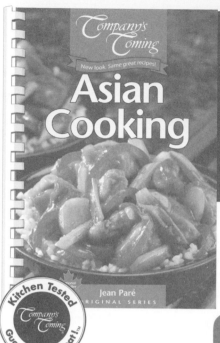
Try it

a sample recipe from *Asian Cooking*

Minty Pawpaw Salad

Asian Cooking, Page 116

DRESSING

Lemon (or lime) juice	2 tbsp.	30 mL
Garlic clove, minced	1	1
(or 1/4 tsp., 1 mL, powder)		
Finely grated gingerroot,	1/2 tsp.	2 mL
(or 1/8 tsp. 0.5 mL, ground ginger)		
Fish sauce	2 tbsp.	30 mL
Golden corn (or cane) syrup	1 tbsp.	15 mL
Chili sauce	1 tbsp.	15 mL
Dried crushed chilies	1/8 tsp.	0.5 mL
Ripe large papayas, peeled, seeded and diced	2	2
Small red onion, cut into paper-thin slices	1	1
Small red pepper, slivered	1	1
Fresh mint leaves, chopped	1/3 cup	75 mL
Butter lettuce leaves	12 - 20	12 - 20

Dressing: Combine first 7 ingredients in small dish. Let stand at room temperature for 30 minutes to blend flavours. Makes 1/3 cup (75 mL) dressing.

Place papaya, onion, red pepper, mint and dressing in large bowl. Toss gently until well coated. Makes 4 cups (1 L) salad.

Line small bowls with 3 to 5 lettuce leaves each. Add 1 cup (250 mL) salad to each. Serves 4.

1 serving: 104 Calories; 0.4 g Total Fat; 539 mg Sodium; 3 g Protein; 25 g Carbohydrate; 4 g Dietary Fibre

If you like what we've done with **cooking**, you'll **love** what we do with **crafts**!